REFERENCE
ONLY

100 More Research Topic Guides for Students

Recent Titles in
Greenwood Professional Guides in School Librarianship

Collaborations for Literacy: Creating an Integrated Language Arts Program for Middle Schools
Rochelle B. Senator

How to Teach about American Indians: A Guide for the School Library Media Specialist
Karen D. Harvey with Lisa D. Harjo and Lynda Welborn

100 Research Topic Guides for Students
Barbara Wood Borne

Special Events Programs in School Library Media Centers: A Guide to Making Them Work
Marcia Trotta

Information Services for Secondary Schools
Dana McDougald and Melvin Bowie

The Internet and the School Library Media Specialist: Transforming Traditional Services
Randall M. MacDonald

Creating a Local Area Network in the School Library Media Center
Becky R. Mather

Collection Assessment and Management for School Libraries: Preparing for Cooperative Collection Development
Debra E. Kachel

Using Educational Technology with At-Risk Students: A Guide for Library Media Specialists and Teachers
Roxanne Baxter Mendrinos

Teaching Electronic Literacy: A Concepts-Based Approach for School Library Media Specialists
Kathleen W. Craver

Block Scheduling and Its Impact on the School Library Media Center
Marie Keen Shaw

Using Internet Primary Sources to Teach Critical Thinking Skills in History
Kathleen W. Craver

100 More Research Topic Guides for Students

DANA McDOUGALD

Greenwood Professional Guides in School Librarianship
Harriet Selverstone, Series Adviser

GREENWOOD PRESS
Westport, Connecticut • London

Library of Congress Cataloging-in-Publication Data

McDougald, Dana, 1942–
    100 more research topic guides for students / Dana McDougald.
      p. cm.—(Greenwood professional guides in school
librarianship, ISSN 1074–150X)
    Follow up to: 100 research topic guides for students / Barbara
Wood Borne.
    Includes bibliographical references and index.
    ISBN 0–313–30852–7 (alk. paper)
    1. Library research—United States.   2. Report writing.
I. Borne, Barbara Wood, 1945–   100 research topic guides for
students. II. Title.   III. Title: One hundred more research topic
guides for students.   IV. Series.
Z710.M19   1999
025.5′24—dc21   99–17855

British Library Cataloguing in Publication Data is available.

Library of Congress Catalog Card Number: 99–17855
ISBN: 0–313–30852–7
ISSN: 1074–150X

First published in 1999

Greenwood Press, 88 Post Road West, Westport, CT 06881
An imprint of Greenwood Publishing Group, Inc.
www.greenwood.com

Printed in the United States of America

The paper used in this book complies with the
Permanent Paper Standard issued by the National
Information Standards Organization (Z39.48–1984).

10 9 8 7 6 5 4 3 2 1

Contents

Contents   vii

Introduction

This book was written in response to the positive reaction to the first edition, *100 Research Topic Guides for Students* by Barbara Wood Borne. Secondary school teachers are making more efforts than ever before to integrate research skills into the curriculum. Students are being required to do reports and projects which necessitate library research in nearly all of their classes. Students and teachers alike welcome guidance on topics and procedures. The purpose of this book is to offer both.

Information literacy is the ability to access, evaluate, and use information from a variety of sources. Students need help in formulating research questions to help them understand exactly what information they are seeking. Presented with a broad topic, such as "Colonial America," students often say, "I want to find everything I can about this topic." It is our job as teachers and librarians to teach students to define what they want to know about the topic in a few sentences or questions, so that their task will not become overwhelming, if not impossible. A teacher or librarian can help a student narrow the topic to "family life in Colonial America," then formulate some questions such as "What did the families do in their leisure time for entertainment?" or "How was food prepared in a typical Colonial American home?" This book provides suggestions for narrowing each topic.

Today libraries have a wide range and variety of information sources: standard books, reference books, periodicals, indexes, CD-ROM encyclopedias and databases, networked indexes and databases, videotapes and filmstrips, vertical file materials, and the Internet. How does a student decide where to begin a search for information? This book offers a systematic method of conducting a search that can apply to almost any topic in almost any library. The research topic guides, or pathfinders, present a logical approach to information searches. When a student learns to search systematically and logically, no library, regardless of size, should be intimidating.

How to Use This Book

100 More Research Topic Guides for Students follows the same basic format as the first edition, *100 Research Topic Guides for Students*. The topics chosen are typical of topics either assigned to or chosen by secondary school students. The guides are "pathfinders" or "infinite bibliographies," designed to help students approach an information search in a logical manner. As a student goes through a search using such a guide, he/she not only learns about appropriate procedures for library research, but also learns about the wide variety of resources available for information.

RESEARCH TOPIC GUIDE FORMAT

Following is a brief explanation of each component of the format of each topic guide.

Topic

Collaboration between media specialist and classroom teacher to integrate information literacy into the curriculum allows students to obtain a wide variety of experiences and opportunities to seek and use information. In this edition are topics that are typically assigned to or chosen by students.

Topics are arranged under five broad areas: Fine Arts, Language Arts, and Foreign Language; Math, Science, and Technology; Social Studies: History, Economics, and Political Science; Social Issues; and Biography. An effort was made to include something from every curricular area found in most secondary schools. Social issues were selected for either their newsworthiness (such as cloning, euthanasia or food safety) or their appeal to teenagers (such as gender roles, runaways, or television talk shows). Biographies include historical figures such as Alexander the Great, Joan of Arc, or a U.S. President of the student's choosing; people who have made important contributions to society in special areas, such as Louis Pasteur or W.E.B. Du Bois; or once-newsworthy people whose legends will not die, such as Princess Diana or Elvis Presley.

Background

A brief introduction to a topic offers background information or definition of a topic.

Look under the Following Subjects in the Library Catalog

Sears List of Subject Headings, 15th edition, is used to suggest headings for the catalog search. *Sears* headings are typically used in school and small public libraries.

Browse for Books on the Shelf Using These Call Numbers

The Dewey Decimal classification system is used because it is typically used in school and small public libraries. Students should be urged to browse the shelves in areas where they have found a reference via the catalog search, because books on a subject are generally shelved in the same area. This section of the guide, in some cases, allows students other choices besides those identified through the catalog search because of the approach that may be taken on a subject.

Reference Material That May Help (Books or CD-ROMs)

Students should search the reference section, using the same call numbers as given above. However, the titles chosen for this section seemed particularly appropriate for the selected topic. While not all libraries will have all titles, students with access to more than one library, or to a library with interlibrary loan privileges, may be able to locate those that seem especially useful.

Periodical Indexes

There are scores of indexes in a wide variety of formats. Those chosen to include in these guides are more typically found in school and small public libraries. They are listed in alphabetical order.

Suggested Internet Sites

One of the positive aspects of using the Internet is the currency of material available; one of the more interesting aspects of using the Internet is the uncertainty that what is there today will still be there tomorrow. Every effort was made to include "stable" sites from reliable sources (such as the Library of Congress, the Smithsonian Institute, or PBS). Students must take the greatest care in typing an URL; each is case sensitive, and must be typed exactly as it appears. Librarians and teachers may want to try to access the suggested Internet sites before the students do, and bookmark those that seem particularly useful.

Key Words for Periodical and Online Searches

Key words and descriptors suggested here are those that the author actually used to find the most useful periodical and online information on the topics. They are listed alphabetically.

Video Programs Related to This Topic

Not all students learn in the same manner, and not any one format is necessarily the most appropriate for information. In an effort to provide students with a variety of information formats, suggested video programs are included. As with the suggested reference books and periodical indexes, not all libraries will have all titles.

Organizations to Contact for Additional Information

Sometimes it is best to go directly to the "source" for information. Students seeking information on a country, for example, might contact an embassy or even a travel agent to obtain up-to-date and useful information. Every effort was made to include a national or international organization with each topic guide. In cases where there was not an appropriate organization, this section was omitted.

Suggestions for Narrowing This Topic

One reason that students have so much trouble doing research is that they find it difficult to narrow or define a topic. The suggestions provided in this section are intended to help students with this process. An effort was made to include nontraditional report methods such as timelines, video creations, and charts as well as the traditional research paper. An effort was also made to suggest thought-provoking projects using comparisons or "what ifs," as well as straight "research and report." It is hoped that the suggestions in this section will inspire students to think of other ways to look at and narrow the topics, as well as help them to think creatively about other topics in the future.

Related Topics

These suggestions provide other topic choices similar to the topic in the present guide, but which offer alternatives that may be more appealing to a student. They are also alternatives for the teacher who prefers that not everyone in the class does the same topic, but similar topics.

Disclaimer

In this section, students are reminded that not all resources suggested will be available in every library, nor are they the only sources with appropriate information for a topic. Students are urged to ask a librarian when needing assistance.

USING RESEARCH TOPIC GUIDES WITH STUDENTS

It is helpful to go over a topic guide with students before they begin their research. At this time locations of resources can be pointed out, or demonstrations of resources, especially electronic or computerized resources, can be given. This is often an excellent opportunity to reinforce how to use the library's computerized catalog or a networked index such as *InfoTrac*.

NOTE

The publisher grants permission to the reader to photocopy an individual topic guide for research purposes.

I

Fine Arts, Language Arts, and Foreign Languages

Architecture

BACKGROUND

Architecture is the art and profession of designing buildings and dates back to more than 5,000 years ago in Mesopotamia and Egypt. The architecture of a place or time period is an important element of the culture of that time or place and the people who lived there.

LOOK UNDER THE FOLLOWING SUBJECTS IN THE LIBRARY CATALOG

> Architecture
> Building
> House Construction
> Modern Architecture

BROWSE FOR BOOKS ON THE SHELF USING THESE CALL NUMBERS

> 690 (Buildings)
> 720–728 (Architecture)

REFERENCE MATERIALS THAT MAY HELP (BOOKS OR CD-ROMS)

> Burden, Ernest. *Illustrated Dictionary of Architecture*. McGraw-Hill, 1998.
> Courtenay-Thompson, Fiona, ed. *The Visual Dictionary of Buildings*. Dorling Kindersley, 1993.
> Sharp, Dennis. *Twentieth Century Architecture: A Visual History*. Facts on File, 1991.
> West, Shearer, ed. *The Bulfinch Guide to Art History: A Comprehensive Survey and Dictionary of Western Art and Architecture*. Little Brown, 1996.
> *World Book's Information Finder*. World Book, date varies. (CD-ROM)

PERIODICAL INDEXES

> *EBSCO Magazine Article Summaries*
> Index to *History Today* Magazine
> *InfoTrac*
> *Reader's Guide to Periodical Literature*

SUGGESTED INTERNET SITES

> http://wwar.world-arts-resources.com/architecture (A resource page that leads you to thousands of architecture-oriented sites)
> http://hyperion.advanced.org/10098/ (Architecture through the ages)

http://www.fswarchitects.com/links.html (Hotlinks to 19th- and 20th-century architecture and design)

KEY WORDS FOR PERIODICAL AND ONLINE SEARCHES

Architects
Architecture
Buildings
House Construction

Use the term "Architecture" and the name of the country or time period that you have chosen to research.

VIDEO PROGRAMS RELATED TO THIS TOPIC

American Art and Architecture. Alarion. list-mail@libsonline.com
The American House. Learning Seed, 1993.
Art of the Western World: From Ancient Greece to Post-Modernism Series (4 video set). PBS.

ORGANIZATIONS TO CONTACT FOR ADDITIONAL INFORMATION

American Architectural Foundation, 1735 New York Avenue, NW, Washington, DC 20006.
Boston Foundation for Architecture, 52 Broad Street, Boston, MA 02109.
Society of Architectural Historians, Chamley-Persky House, 1365 North Astor Street, Chicago, IL 60610–2144. Phone: 312–573–1365. http://www.sah.org

SUGGESTIONS FOR NARROWING THIS TOPIC

Discuss how climate influences architectural design. Focus on three parts of the world with very different climates.
Discuss structures of Ancient Rome: Colosseum, The Forum of Caesar, The Circus Maximus, and The Pantheon.
Discuss architectural access for the handicapped.

RELATED TOPICS

Animal Habitats and Their Influence upon Architectural Design
Environmental Design
Landscape Architecture
Stonehenge as an Architectural Structure

This RESEARCH TOPIC GUIDE is intended to help you find information on your topic in a wide variety of sources in this and any other library. Resources, though, are not limited to those described and not all libraries will have the same titles. Please ask a librarian for further guidance.

Arthurian Legends

BACKGROUND

King Arthur, legendary king of early Britons, has been inspiration for countless novels, poems, stories, plays, and motion pictures. According to legend, he was born to King Uther Pendragon and Duchess Igraine of Cornwall, raised by Sir Ector, one of Uther's barons, and guided by Merlin the Magician after he proved himself to be the rightful heir to the throne of Briton.

LOOK UNDER THE FOLLOWING SUBJECTS IN THE LIBRARY CATALOG

    Arthurian Romances
    Chivalry
    Knights and Knighthood
    Middle Ages

BROWSE FOR BOOKS ON THE SHELF USING THESE CALL NUMBERS

    394 (Customs of Chivalry)
    398.22 (Tales of Heroes)
    929.7 (Orders of Knighthood)

REFERENCE MATERIALS THAT MAY HELP (BOOKS OR CD-ROMS)

    The Arthurian Tradition. Films for the Humanities and Sciences, 1998. (CD-ROM)
    Bulfinch, Thomas and Norma Lorre Goodrich. *Bulfinch's Mythology: The Age of Chivalry and Legends of Charlemagne or Romance in the Middle Ages.* Penguin, 1995.
    Coghlan, Ronan. *The Illustrated Encyclopaedia of Arthurian Legends.* Element Books Ltd., 1993.
    Day, David. *The Search for King Arthur.* Facts on File, 1995.

PERIODICAL INDEXES

    EBSCO Magazine Article Summaries
    Index to *History Today* Magazine
    InfoTrac
    Reader's Guide to Periodical Literature

SUGGESTED INTERNET SITES

    http://www.britannia.com/history/arthur (A guide to the extensive resources available in Britannia's King Arthur Department)
    http://www.georgetown.edu/labyrinth/subjects/arthurian/arthur.html (Resources for Arthurian Studies)

http://dc.smu.edu/Arthuriana (Home page of the scholarly journal about King Arthur)

http://www.lib.montana.edu/~slainte/arthur (Arthurian resources on the Internet)

KEY WORDS FOR PERIODICAL AND ONLINE SEARCHES

Arthurian Romances
King Arthur
Knights and Knighthood
Romances

VIDEO PROGRAMS RELATED TO THIS TOPIC

King Arthur: His Life and Legends. A & E, 1995.
Le Morte d'Arthur. Films for the Humanities and Sciences, 1993.
The Legend of Arthur. Films for the Humanities and Sciences, 1985.
The True Legend of King Arthur. Films for the Humanities and Sciences, 1993.

ORGANIZATIONS TO CONTACT FOR ADDITIONAL INFORMATION

International Arthurian Society—North American Branch, c/o Joan Grimbert, Treasurer, Department of Modern Languages and Literatures, Catholic University, Washington, DC 20064.

Oxford Arthurian Society, c/o Hannah Means, Regent's Park College, Oxford, OX1 2LB.

SUGGESTIONS FOR NARROWING THIS TOPIC

Discuss both pros and cons for the existence of King Arthur.

Prepare a pictorial report, with captions, of clothing worn during the age of King Arthur. Include the clothing of all classes of people, including knights.

Research the origins of the Arthurian legend.

What is the "Code of Chivalry?" Compare and contrast this code with the actual life of a typical knight.

RELATED TOPICS

Holy Grail
Heraldry
Round Table

This RESEARCH TOPIC GUIDE is intended to help you find information on your topic in a wide variety of sources in this and any other library. Resources, though, are not limited to those described and not all libraries will have the same titles. Please ask a librarian for further guidance.

Bonsai

BACKGROUND

Bonsai, the art of growing trees in a confined space such as a pot or tray, has its origins in China as early as the 1000s A.D. Its popularity spread to Japan and eventually worldwide. The object of bonsai is to create a small tree with all of the characteristics of a large tree in nature. It is a hobby that holds much fascination both to those who practice it and to those who merely observe the fruits of others' labors.

LOOK UNDER THE FOLLOWING SUBJECTS IN THE LIBRARY CATALOG

Bonsai

Dwarf Trees

Trees

BROWSE FOR BOOKS ON THE SHELF USING THESE CALL NUMBERS

582.16 (Trees)

635.9 (Flowers and Ornamental Plants)

REFERENCE MATERIALS THAT MAY HELP (BOOKS OR CD-ROMS)

Complete Gardening. Microsoft, n.d. (CD-ROM)

Giorgi, Gianfranco. *Simon and Schuster's Guide to Bonsai*. Simon and Schuster Books, 1991.

Koreshoff, Deborah R. *Bonsai: Its Art, Science, History and Philosophy*. Timber Press, 1997.

Naka, John, Hideo Aragaki, and John Bester (Translator). *Classic Bonsai of Japan*. Kodansha International, 1989.

Tomlinson, Harry and Elvin McDonald. *The Complete Book of Bonsai*. Abbeville Press, 1991.

PERIODICAL INDEXES

EBSCO Magazine Article Summaries

InfoTrac

Reader's Guide to Periodical Literature

SUGGESTED INTERNET SITES

http://www.absbonsai.org (Home page of the American Bonsai Society)

http://interzone.ucc.ie/98/marley/bonsai.htm (Directions for starting and growing a bonsai tree)

http://www.weyerhaeuser.com/bonsai/ (Pacific Rim Bonsai collection) http://www.mmjp.or.jp/mini-bonsai/ (The world of mini-bonsai)

http://www.bonsaiweb.com/ (A web site devoted to the study of the ancient art of bonsai)

KEY WORDS FOR PERIODICAL AND ONLINE SEARCHES

Aboriculture

Bonsai

Chinese Gardens

Japanese Gardens

VIDEO PROGRAMS RELATED TO THIS TOPIC

Basic Bonsai Care "1." Bob Johnston, RD 1, Box 370, Tarentum, PA 15084.

Bonsai Basics Series (5 videos). Japan: *Bonsai World Magazine*, 1995. Distributed by New Planning USA, 4431 Corporate Center Drive, Suite 115, Los Alamitos, CA 90720–2500.

ORGANIZATIONS TO CONTACT FOR ADDITIONAL INFORMATION

The American Bonsai Society. http://www.absbonsai.org (From this site, one can obtain names and addresses of clubs in all of the states of the United States and Canada.)

Bonsai Club International, P.O. Box 1176, Brookfield, WI 53008–1176.

Internet Bonsai Club. http://www.geocities.com/Tokyo/Garden/6895

SUGGESTIONS FOR NARROWING THIS TOPIC

Relate the history and basic techniques of bonsai.

Describe, discuss, and either draw or find pictures of the five basic styles of bonsai.

RELATED TOPICS

Ikebana

Pond and Water Gardening

Suiseki

Symbolism and Meaning in Japanese Gardens

This RESEARCH TOPIC GUIDE is intended to help you find information on your topic in a wide variety of sources in this and any other library. Resources, though, are not limited to those described and not all libraries will have the same titles. Please ask a librarian for further guidance.

Countries of the World

BACKGROUND

To learn more about a country and its people is an essential aspect of the study of another language. Some languages such as French are spoken in more than one country or, like Spanish, spoken in many countries. Choose a country where the foreign language that you are studying is spoken and find out more about it. An excellent starting place for researching a country and its people is *World Book Encyclopedia* and the index to *National Geographic Magazine*.

LOOK UNDER THE FOLLOWING SUBJECTS IN THE LIBRARY CATALOG

Search under the name of the country you have selected to research. The catalog may provide references to related topics (example: Mexico—See also Indians of Mexico).

BROWSE FOR BOOKS ON THE SHELF USING THESE CALL NUMBERS

910–919 (Geography and Travel)

940–998 (General Histories of Countries)

When you locate a book on your country after a catalog search, search the shelves in the same area as that book. You will probably find more books on the country.

REFERENCE MATERIALS THAT MAY HELP (BOOKS OR CD-ROMS)

Clapson, Debra, et al., eds. *The Dorling Kindersley World Reference Atlas*. DK Publishing, 1996.

Famighetti, Robert, ed. *The World Almanac and Book of Facts*. St. Martin's Press, annual.

Hunter, Brian, ed. *The Statesman's Year-Book*. St. Martin's Press, date varies.

Lands and Peoples. Grolier Education Corporation, 1997.

Philip, George. *Encyclopedic World Atlas*. Oxford University Press, 1997.

Rand McNally World Vista. Rand McNally, 1996. (CD-ROM)

PERIODICAL INDEXES

EBSCO Magazine Article Summaries

Index to *National Geographic Magazine*

InfoTrac

Reader's Guide to Periodical Literature

SUGGESTED INTERNET SITES

http://www.fodors.com (Fodor's travel online)

http://www.odci.gov/cia/publications/factbook/index.html (CIA's World Factbook online)

http://www.theodora.com/flags.html (Flags of all countries)

http://www.countries.com/ (Lists over 200 countries, with statistical data and links to culture, travel, weather, government, and more)

KEY WORDS FOR PERIODICAL AND ONLINE SEARCHES

Search under the name of the country you are researching. Periodical indexes will have a number of cross references for articles about your country such as culture, economic conditions, description and travel, foreign relations, industry, politics and government, etcetera.

VIDEO PROGRAMS RELATED TO THIS TOPIC

European Geography Series. Encyclopaedia Britannica, 1993.
The Regions of Africa. Encyclopaedia Britannica, 1993.
The Sights and Sounds of South America. Video Knowledge, 1997.
Windows to the World: Asia (4 videos: China, India, Japan, Thailand). IVN Communications, 1996.

ORGANIZATIONS TO CONTACT FOR ADDITIONAL INFORMATION

International Association of Convention and Visitor Bureaus, 2000 L Street, NW, Suite 702, Washington, DC 20036–4990. http://www.iacvb. org/iacvb.html

World Tourism Organization, Capitan Haya, 42, 28020 Madrid, Spain. http://omtweb@world-tourism.org

SUGGESTIONS FOR NARROWING THIS TOPIC

Create a travel brochure for the country you are researching. Include basic historical, cultural, and geographical facts. Provide information such as where to stay, where to eat, sightseeing highlights, and travel tips.

Provide information on the cultural arts of a country of your choice, including art, music, and literature.

Report on the country of your choice, providing information on the land and its resources, lifestyles of the people, government, and historical data.

RELATED TOPICS

Development of the Language You Are Studying
Flag(s) of the Country You Are Studying, including History and Symbolism
Wildlife of the Country You Are Studying

This RESEARCH TOPIC GUIDE is intended to help you find information on your topic in a wide variety of sources in this and any other library. Resources, though, are not limited to those described and not all libraries will have the same titles. Please ask a librarian for further guidance.

Creation Myths

BACKGROUND

Creation stories, or creation myths, date from the earliest man's attempts to explain the mysteries of nature and the universe. Amazingly, creation myths, regardless of their origins, tend to have similar themes running through them, such as the idea of an initially formless universe from which order was brought. Other themes include the separation of the sky and earth and the creation of human beings at some stage by gods or other supernatural beings.

LOOK UNDER THE FOLLOWING SUBJECTS IN THE LIBRARY CATALOG

Bible and Science
Creation
Creationism
Mythology

BROWSE FOR BOOKS ON THE SHELF USING THESE CALL NUMBERS

215 (Science and Religion)
231.7 (Creation)
398 (Folklore)

REFERENCE MATERIALS THAT MAY HELP (BOOKS OR CD-ROMS)

Encyclopedia of Religion. Macmillan Library Reference USA, 1987.
Encyclopedia of World Cultures. Macmillan Library Reference USA, 1998. (CD-ROM)
Leeming, David Adams. *A Dictionary of Creation Myths.* Oxford University Press, 1996.
Leeming, David Adams. *Encyclopedia of Creation Myths.* ABC-CLIO, 1994.
Sproul, Barbara C. *Primal Myths: Creation Myths around the World.* Harper, San Francisco, 1992.
VonFranz, Marie-Luise. *Creation Myths.* Shambhala, 1995.

PERIODICAL INDEXES

EBSCO Magazine Article Summaries
InfoTrac
Reader's Guide to Periodical Literature

SUGGESTED INTERNET SITES

http://www.dc.peachnet.edu/~shale/humanities/literature/religion/creation.html (Creation myths from around the world)
http://www.magictails.com (An illustrated series of original creation myths)

KEY WORDS FOR PERIODICAL AND ONLINE SEARCHES
Comparative Religion
Creation
Folklore
Mythology

VIDEO PROGRAMS RELATED TO THIS TOPIC
Mythology Lives: Ancient Stories and Modern Literature. Guidance Association, 1986.
The Power of Myth. Mystic Fire/Voyager, 1988.
The World Religions: 600 BC–AD 500. Network Television.

ORGANIZATION TO CONTACT FOR ADDITIONAL INFORMATION
The Association of Cultural Mythologists, 19072 Mathew Circle, Huntington Beach, CA 92646. lugaro2000@aol.com.

SUGGESTIONS FOR NARROWING THIS TOPIC
Compare three to five creation myths from different cultures, discussing recurring themes and other similarities.
How do theories of creation in creation myths differ and/or compare with scientific theories of evolution?
Compare three creation myths from different cultures with the Biblical story of creation.

RELATED TOPICS
Ancient Religions
Gods and Goddesses
Religion vs. Science

This RESEARCH TOPIC GUIDE is intended to help you find information on your topic in a wide variety of sources in this and any other library. Resources, though, are not limited to those described and not all libraries will have the same titles. Please ask a librarian for further guidance.

Fairy Tales

BACKGROUND

Today, fairy tales are regarded as stories told primarily to children, yet these stories were not originally intended for children (see http://www.darkgoddess.com/fairy). Women told these stories as a means of communicating their frustrations with their lot in society and life in general. Not until writers like the Grimm Brothers and Hans Christian Andersen began writing fairy tales was this type of story included in children's literature.

LOOK UNDER THE FOLLOWING SUBJECTS IN THE LIBRARY CATALOG

Children's Literature
Fairy Tales
Fantasy Fiction
Literature

BROWSE FOR BOOKS ON THE SHELF USING THESE CALL NUMBERS

398.21 (Fairy Tales)
808.83 (Collections of Tales)
813 (American Fiction)
823 (English Fiction)

REFERENCE MATERIALS THAT MAY HELP (BOOKS OR CD-ROMS)

Bettelheim, Bruno. *The Uses of Enchantment: The Meaning and Importance of Fairy Tales*. Vintage Books, 1989.
Favorite Fairy Tales. Queue, 1994. (CD-ROM)
Hearne, Betsy. *Beauties and Beasts* (*The Oryx Multicultural Folktale Series*). Oryx Press, 1993.
Jones, Steven S. *Fairy Tale: The Magic Mirror of Imagination*. Twayne, 1995.
Zipes, Jack. *Fairy Tale as Myth; Myth as Fairy Tale*. University Press of Kentucky, 1994.
Zipes, Jack, ed. *Spells of Enchantment: The Wondrous Fairy Tales of Western Culture*. Penguin, 1992.

PERIODICAL INDEXES

EBSCO Magazine Article Summaries
InfoTrac
Reader's Guide to Periodical Literature

SUGGESTED INTERNET SITES

http://www.darkgoddess.com/fairy (Origins and evolution of the fairy tale) http://www.math.technion.ac.il/~rl/Andersen (A collection of Hans Christian Andersen's fairy tales and stories)

http://www.cln.org/themes/fairytales.html (Links to fairy tales, resources, and lesson plans)

KEY WORDS FOR PERIODICAL AND ONLINE SEARCHES

Children's Literature

Fairy Tales

Folklore and Children

Symbolism in Fairy Tales

Also search under names of particular fairy tales, such as: *Cinderella*, *Beauty and the Beast*, or *Hansel and Gretel.*

VIDEO PROGRAMS RELATED TO THIS TOPIC

Encyclopedia Britannica; Fairytales from around the World Series. Britannica, 1992. (Available from Library Video.)

From the Brothers Grimm (a series of 10 videos). (Available from Filmic Archives.)

Mother Goose Video Treasury, 1991. (Available from Library Video.)

ORGANIZATION TO CONTACT FOR ADDITIONAL INFORMATION

The National Council for the Traditional Arts, 1320 Fenwick Lane, Suite 200, Silver Spring, MD 20910.

SUGGESTIONS FOR NARROWING THIS TOPIC

Discuss the differences between fairy tales, myths, and folk tales.

Discuss the evolution of the fairy tale.

Discuss three elements common to most fairy tales. Provide examples from a wide variety of tales.

RELATED TOPICS

Development of Children's Literature

Mother Goose

Nursery Rhymes

This RESEARCH TOPIC GUIDE is intended to help you find information on your topic in a wide variety of sources in this and any other library. Resources, though, are not limited to those described and not all libraries will have the same titles. Please ask a librarian for further guidance.

Globe Theatre

BACKGROUND

The Globe Theatre was built in 1599 by Richard and Cuthbert Burbage from materials their father had used to build a theatre in 1576. It was in this theatre that Shakespeare's acting company, called the Chamberlain's Men, performed his plays. It burned in 1613 during a performance of *Henry VIII*, but was rebuilt the following year, where it remained until it was closed in 1642 and pulled down two years later.

LOOK UNDER THE FOLLOWING SUBJECTS IN THE LIBRARY CATALOG

> English Drama
> Globe Theatre (Southwark, England)
> Shakespeare, William
> Theater—History

BROWSE FOR BOOKS ON THE SHELF USING THESE CALL NUMBERS

> 792 (Theater)
> 822.3 (Shakespeare)

REFERENCE MATERIALS THAT MAY HELP (BOOKS OR CD-ROMS)

> Brown, John Russell. *Shakespeare and His Theatre*. William Morrow & Co., 1982.
> *DISCovering Shakespeare*. Gale Research, 1995.
> Morley, Jacqueline. *Shakespeare's Theatre: Inside Story*. Peter Bedrick Books, 1994.
> *Shakespeare and the Globe Theatre*. Learning Tomorrow, n.d. (CD-ROM)
> *Shakespeare's Life and Times*. Intellimation, 1994. (CD-ROM)
> Thomson, Peter. *Shakespeare's Theatre*. Routledge, 1992.

PERIODICAL INDEXES

> *EBSCO Magazine Article Summaries*
> Index to *History Today* Magazine
> *InfoTrac*
> *Reader's Guide to Periodical Literature*

SUGGESTED INTERNET SITES

> http://shakespeares-globe.org/ (Extensive information about the Globe)
> http://www.uga.edu/~sgc-se/ (The architecture of the new Globe Theatre and the promotion of Shakespeare in education)
> http://falcon.jmu.edu/~ramseyil/shakes.htm (A variety of Shakespeare resources on the web)

http://www.sorcom.com/~creative/globe/netscape/index.html (History of
the Globe Theatre)

KEY WORDS FOR PERIODICAL AND ONLINE SEARCHES

Elizabethan Theatre
Globe Theatre (Southwark, London)
Shakespeare, William
Theatre History

VIDEO PROGRAMS RELATED TO THIS TOPIC

Shakespeare: A Day at the Globe. Guidance Association.
Shakespeare and His Theatre: The Globe. Films for the Humanities and Sciences, 1993.
Shakespeare and the Globe. Films for the Humanities and Sciences, 1984.

ORGANIZATIONS TO CONTACT FOR ADDITIONAL INFORMATION

International Shakespeare Globe Centre, c/o Susannah Howard, Director, New Globe Walk, Bankside, Southwark, London SE1 9DT, UK. Phone: 071–620–0202, Fax: 071–928–7968.

The Shakespeare Programme, c/o Professor Lawrence Opitz, Director, Department of Theatre, Skidmore College, Saratoga Springs, NY 12866–1632. Phone: 518–580–5432, Fax: 518–584–7963.

SUGGESTIONS FOR NARROWING THIS TOPIC

Create a model of the Globe Theatre.
Research the history of the original Globe Theatre in Southwark, London.
Research the history of the rebuilding of the Globe Theatre, a project which began in 1987.

RELATED TOPICS

Costumes of the Elizabethan Theater
Elizabethan Theater (History)
Life of actors in Elizabethan Theater
Origins of Theater

This RESEARCH TOPIC GUIDE is intended to help you find information on your topic in a wide variety of sources in this and any other library. Resources, though, are not limited to those described and not all libraries will have the same titles. Please ask a librarian for further guidance.

Harlem Renaissance

BACKGROUND

The 1920s and 1930s saw a surge of creativity in the African American community, particulary in literature, art, and music. Because this creativity began as a series of literary discussions in the Greenwich Village and Harlem sections of New York, the movement, which focused on the African American's place in American life, has become known as the Harlem Renaissance.

LOOK UNDER THE FOLLOWING SUBJECTS IN THE LIBRARY CATALOG

> African American Art
>
> African American Music
>
> American Literature—African American Authors
>
> Harlem Renaissance

Also search under names of particular authors, artists, or musicians (examples: Cullen, Countee; Hughes, Langston).

BROWSE FOR BOOKS ON THE SHELF USING THESE CALL NUMBERS

> 704 (African American Art)
>
> 780.089 (African American Music)
>
> 810.9 (American Literature: history, description, critical appraisal)
>
> 974.7 (New York)

REFERENCE MATERIALS THAT MAY HELP (BOOKS OR CD-ROMS)

> *African American History: Slavery to Civil Rights.* Queue/Clearvue, 1994. (CD-ROM)
>
> *Black American Poets and Dramatists of the Harlem Renaissance.* Chelsea House, 1995.
>
> *Black American Prose Writers of the Harlem Renaissance.* Chelsea House, 1994.
>
> *Cultural Contributions of Black Americans.* Clearvue, 1995. (CD-ROM)
>
> Driskell, David C., et al., eds. *Harlem Renaissance: Art of Black America.* Abradale/Abrams, 1994.
>
> Haskins, James. *The Harlem Renaissance.* The Millbrook Press, 1996.

PERIODICAL INDEXES

> *EBSCO Magazine Article Summaries*
>
> *InfoTrac*
>
> *Reader's Guide to Periodical Literature*

SUGGESTED INTERNET SITES

> http://www.csustan.edu/english/reuben/pal/chap9/chap9.html (Perspectives in American Literature: A Research and Reference Guide: Chapter 9: Harlem Renaissance)

http://www.geocities.com/Athens/Forum/4722/big.html (Harlem Renaissance: Poetry, Politics, Women, Jazz, Theater)

http://www.msstate.edu/Archives/History/USA/Afro-Amer/afro.html (African American History website)

http://www.nku.edu/~diesmanj/harlem.html (Collections of poetry from Langston Hughes and others; links to other sites of the period)

KEY WORDS FOR PERIODICAL AND ONLINE SEARCHES

African American Literature

African American Studies

Harlem (New York)

Harlem Renaissance

VIDEO PROGRAMS RELATED TO THIS TOPIC

African American Art: Past and Present. Reading and O'Reilly, 1992.

Lorraine Hansberry: The Black Experience in the Creation of Drama. Films for the Humanities and Sciences, 1975.

Tryin' to Get Home: A History of African American Song. Heebie Jeebie Music, 1993.

ORGANIZATIONS TO CONTACT FOR ADDITIONAL INFORMATION

Association for the Study of Afro-American Life and History, c/o Mrs. Irena Webster, Executive Director, 1407 14th Street, N.W., Washington, DC 20005.

Circle Brotherhood Association, c/o Henry Curtis III. http://HCURTISIII@aol.com

SUGGESTIONS FOR NARROWING THIS TOPIC

Discuss the importance of the Harlem Renaissance as a social as well as a cultural movement.

Select an author, artist, or musician of the Harlem Renaissance and prepare a paper on his/her life and works.

RELATED TOPICS

African Americans and Politics

Civil Rights Movement

Protest Literature (African Americans)

School Integration

This RESEARCH TOPIC GUIDE is intended to help you find information on your topic in a wide variety of sources in this and any other library. Resources, though, are not limited to those described and not all libraries will have the same titles. Please ask a librarian for further guidance.

Kabuki

BACKGROUND

Kabuki is a traditional Japanese theatrical art, dating back to the 1600s, which is performed entirely by male actors. Some of the outstanding features of kabuki include the fabulous sets and costumes, the "mawari butai" (revolving stage), and the "hana-michi," a long, narrow extension of the stage that runs through the audience to the back of the theater.

LOOK UNDER THE FOLLOWING SUBJECTS IN THE LIBRARY CATALOG

Kabuki
Japanese Drama
Theater—Japan

BROWSE FOR BOOKS ON THE SHELF USING THESE CALL NUMBERS

792.0952 (Japanese Theater)
895.6 (Japanese Literature)

REFERENCE MATERIALS THAT MAY HELP (BOOKS OR CD-ROMS)

Ernest, Earie. *Kabuki Theatre*. University of Hawaii Press, 1974.
Leiter, Samuel L. *Art of Kabuki: Famous Plays in Performance*. University of California Press, 1979.
Leiter, Samuel and Jiro Kabuki Jiten Yamamoto. *New Kabuki Encyclopedia: A Revised Adaptation of Kabuki Jiten*. Greenwood, 1997.
Shaver, Ruth M. *Kabuki Costume*. Charles E. Tuttle, 1990.
Young, Margaret. *Kabuki: Japanese Drama*. Eastern Press, 1986.

PERIODICAL INDEXES

EBSCO Magazine Article Summaries
InfoTrac
Reader's Guide to Periodical Literature

SUGGESTED INTERNET SITES

http://www.fix.co.jp/kabuki/ (Kabuki for everyone)
http://webforce.nwrain.net/kabuki/ (Essay and pictures on Kabuki)
http://asnic.utexas.edu/asnic/countries/japan/kabuki.html (Kabuki: Traditional Theatrical Arts—background, repertoire, aesthetic elements, theater and stage, actors, and present-day kabuki)

KEY WORDS FOR PERIODICAL AND ONLINE SEARCHES

Japanese Drama
Kabuki
Kabuki Plays
Theater

VIDEO PROGRAM RELATED TO THIS TOPIC

Kabuki. Films for the Humanities and Sciences, 1988.

ORGANIZATION TO CONTACT FOR ADDITIONAL INFORMATION

Kabuki Academy. http://kabuki@nwrain.com

SUGGESTION FOR NARROWING THIS TOPIC

Discuss the history and distinguishing features of kabuki.

RELATED TOPICS

Kimono Dressing
Kuma-dori Makeup
Nihon Buyoo (Japanese Dancing)
Shamisen Music

This RESEARCH TOPIC GUIDE is intended to help you find information on your topic in a wide variety of sources in this and any other library. Resources, though, are not limited to those described and not all libraries will have the same titles. Please ask a librarian for further guidance.

Literary Prizes

BACKGROUND

Once an author has achieved the dream of getting his/her work published, the ultimate honor is to be awarded a prize for one's work. For example, the John Newbery Medal, established in 1922, is awarded to the most distinguished contribution to American literature for children, while the Randolph Caldecott Medal, established in 1938, is awarded for the most distinguished American picture book for children.

LOOK UNDER THE FOLLOWING SUBJECTS IN THE LIBRARY CATALOG

Literary Prizes

Literature—Competitions

Also search under names of awards, such as Caldecott Medal or Newbery Medal.

BROWSE FOR BOOKS ON THE SHELF USING THIS CALL NUMBER

807.9 (Literary Prizes)

REFERENCE MATERIALS THAT MAY HELP (BOOKS OR CD-ROMS)

Allen, Ruth. *Children's Book Prizes: An Evaluation and History of Major Awards for Children's Books in the English-Speaking World.* Ashgate, 1998.

Exploring Novels. Gale, 1997. (CD-ROM)

Exploring Poetry. Gale, 1997. (CD-ROM)

Gunther, Ralph. *Giants in their Field: An Introduction to the Nobel Prizes in Literature.* Scripta Humanistica, 1993.

The Newbery and Caldecott Awards: A Guide to the Medal and Honor Books 1998. American Library Association, 1998. (Published annually)

Twaynes Masterwork Studies. Twayne, 1997. (CD-ROM)

PERIODICAL INDEXES

EBSCO Magazine Article Summaries

InfoTrac

Reader's Guide to Periodical Literature

SUGGESTED INTERNET SITES

http://www.ala.org/alsc (American Library Association—lists of literary prizes)

http://www.yahoo.com/Arts/Humanities/Literature/Awards (Links to literary awards)

KEY WORDS FOR PERIODICAL AND ONLINE SEARCHES

Literary Awards

Literary Prizes

Nobel Prizes—Literature

Also search under names of awards, such as Caldecott Award or Newbery Award.

VIDEO PROGRAMS RELATED TO THIS TOPIC

The American Novel. Educational Dimensions. 1990.

Ten Great Writers: The Modern World (10 videocassettes). Films Incorporated, 1998. (Available from Zenger Media.)

ORGANIZATIONS TO CONTACT FOR ADDITIONAL INFORMATION

American Library Association, 50 E. Huron Street, Chicago, IL 70711–2795.

The Swedish Academy, Box 5232, Sturegata 14, S-10245, Stockholm, Sweden.

SUGGESTIONS FOR NARROWING THIS TOPIC

Many state library associations award literary prizes for books by local authors. Name four of those states, describe the awards for literature and the criteria by which the books are judged, and give background information about the books and authors who recently won.

Research the history of a literary prize, such as the Nobel Prize, Randolph Caldecott Medal, John Newbery Medal, National Book Award, etcetera.

Write a biographical essay about Alfred Nobel, covering his life, work, and will.

RELATED TOPICS

Elements of Excellent Fiction

Prizes or Awards in Other Art Related Fields, such as Music or the Visual Arts

This RESEARCH TOPIC GUIDE is intended to help you find information on your topic in a wide variety of sources in this and any other library. Resources, though, are not limited to those described and not all libraries will have the same titles. Please ask a librarian for further guidance.

The Odyssey of Homer

BACKGROUND

Homer, a great poet of ancient Greece, is believed to be the writer of the epic poems *The Iliad* and *The Odyssey*. *The Odyssey* describes the adventures of Odysseus (called Ulysses by the Romans) on his voyage home to Ithaca after the Trojan War. Odysseus is the kind of hero of legend, mythology, and history who has captured the fascination of people since *The Odyssey* was written, probably in the 8th century B.C.

LOOK UNDER THE FOLLOWING SUBJECTS IN THE LIBRARY CATALOG

    Classical Mythology

    Heroes and Heroines

    Legends

    Mythology

BROWSE FOR BOOKS ON THE SHELF USING THESE CALL NUMBERS

    291.1 (Religious Mythology)

    398.22 (Heroes and Heroines)

    883 (Classical Greek Epic Poetry)

REFERENCE MATERIALS THAT MAY HELP (BOOKS OR CD-ROMS)

    Ancient Writers: Greece and Rome. Charles Scribner's Sons, 1982.

    Daly, Kathleen N. *Greek and Roman Mythology A to Z: A Young Reader's Companion*. Facts on File, 1992.

    Senior, Michael. *The Illustrated Who's Who in Mythology*. Macmillan, 1985.

    Severin, Tim. *The Ulysses Voyage: Sea Search for the Odyssey*. E. P. Dutton, 1987.

    The Myths and Legends of Ancient Greece. Clearvue/eav, 1994. (CD-ROM)

    The Voyages of Ulysses and Aeneas. Clearvue/eav, 1994. (CD-ROM)

PERIODICAL INDEXES

    EBSCO Magazine Article Summaries

    InfoTrac

    Reader's Guide to Periodical Literature

SUGGESTED INTERNET SITES

    http://www.mythweb.com/odyssey/ (Both short and detailed accounts of Odysseus; teacher's guide)

    http://classics.mit.edu/index.html (The Internet Classics Archive; 441 works of classical literature) http://www.hyperdrive.com/odyssey/resources.html (Homer's Odyssey resources page)

KEY WORDS FOR PERIODICAL AND ONLINE SEARCHES

Homer
Mythology, Greek
Odysseus (Legendary Character)
The Odyssey

VIDEO PROGRAMS RELATED TO THIS TOPIC

Homer's Mythology: Tracing a Tradition. Guidance Associates.
The Odyssey. Hallmark, 1997.

ORGANIZATIONS TO CONTACT FOR ADDITIONAL INFORMATION

Joseph Campbell Foundation, 1555 Sherman Avenue #111, Evanston, IL 60201.
The National Endowment for the Humanities. http://www.neh.gov/

SUGGESTIONS FOR NARROWING THIS TOPIC

Compare Odysseus to a modern-day hero.
Design a mythology board game based on the adventures of Odysseus as portrayed in *The Odyssey*.
Develop a character sketch of Odysseus as portrayed in *The Odyssey*.
Select a single incident from *The Odyssey* and discuss the significance of the episode for the poem as a whole.

RELATED TOPICS

Daily Life in Ancient Greece
The Iliad
The Trojan War
Women in Greek mythology

This RESEARCH TOPIC GUIDE is intended to help you find information on your topic in a wide variety of sources in this and any other library. Resources, though, are not limited to those described and not all libraries will have the same titles. Please ask a librarian for further guidance.

Oral Tradition in Literature

BACKGROUND

People told stories before words were written, and those stories were passed from generation to generation. Even today, stories are told to children that parents heard from their parents or grandparents. Storytelling is a popular pastime and entertainment today among people of all ages. Stories and oral histories are one way that people learn about the past from those who have experienced it.

LOOK UNDER THE FOLLOWING SUBJECTS IN THE LIBRARY CATALOG

> Folklore
> Nursery Rhymes
> Storytelling

BROWSE FOR BOOKS ON THE SHELF USING THESE CALL NUMBERS

> 372.64 (Storytelling)
> 398.2 (Folk Literature)
> 398.8 (Rhymes and Rhyming Games)
> 808.5 (Storytelling)

REFERENCE MATERIALS THAT MAY HELP (BOOKS OR CD-ROMS)

> Cunningham, Keith and W. K. McNeil. *The Oral Tradition of the American West: Adventure, Courtship, Family, and Place in Traditional Recitation.* August House, 1990.
> Leeming, David Adams, ed. *Storytelling Encyclopedia: Historical, Cultural, and Multiethnic Approaches to Oral Traditions Around the World.* Oryx Press, 1997.
> *Myths of Africa, Arabia, Ireland and Scandinavia.* Clearvue/eav, 1995. (CD-ROM)
> Pellowski, Anne. *The World of Storytelling.* H. W. Wilson, 1990.
> Vansina, Jan. *Oral Tradition As History.* University of Wisconsin Press, 1985.

PERIODICAL INDEXES

> *EBSCO Magazine Article Summaries*
> *InfoTrac*
> *Reader's Guide to Periodical Literature*

SUGGESTED INTERNET SITES

> http://web.missouri.edu/~csottime/info.html (Center for Studies in Oral Tradition)
> http://lcweb.loc.gov/folklife/afc.html (The American Folklife Center: Library of Congress)

http://www.yale.edu/ynhti/curriculum/units/1984/4/ (Yale-New Haven Teachers' Institute: The Oral Tradition)

http://www.mediahistory.com/oral.html (The Media History Project Connections Page: Oral and scribal culture)

KEY WORDS FOR PERIODICAL AND ONLINE SEARCHES
Folk Literature
Oral History
Oral Tradition (Literature)
Storytelling

VIDEO PROGRAMS RELATED TO THIS TOPIC
American Storytelling Series (8 videocassettes). H. W. Wilson, 1986.
Storytelling with Caroline Feller Bauer. H. W. Wilson, 1986.
Tall Tales & Legends Series (3 videocassettes). (Available from Library Video.)

ORGANIZATIONS TO CONTACT FOR ADDITIONAL INFORMATION
American Folklife Center, Library of Congress, 101 Independence Avenue, SE, Washington, DC 20540–4610.

Center for Studies in Oral Tradition at the University of Missouri—Columbia. http://www.missouri.edu/~csottime/info.html

Vancouver Society of Storytelling, Suite 100, 938 Howe Street, Vancouver, BC, Canada, V6Z 1 N9.

SUGGESTIONS FOR NARROWING THIS TOPIC
Explain oral tradition as a source of history.

Explain how African American slaves used oral tradition to teach their children. Find examples of stories that were told.

Interview one or more persons 75 years or older. Gather examples of stories that they remember having been told to them as children. What did you learn about the past from this experience?

RELATED TOPICS
Fairy Tales
Native American Literature
Nursery Rhymes
Tall Tales

This RESEARCH TOPIC GUIDE is intended to help you find information on your topic in a wide variety of sources in this and any other library. Resources, though, are not limited to those described and not all libraries will have the same titles. Please ask a librarian for further guidance.

Pictorial Symbolism

BACKGROUND

A pictorial symbol is a visual object that stands for or represents or communicates a fact, idea, or another object. Before formal written languages were developed, man used pictorial symbols to represent thoughts and abstract ideas or to tell stories. Religions use pictorial symbolism to represent religious beliefs. Nations use symbols, such as flags and seals. Some people find symbolism in objects, such as flowers or the stars and planets; even colors are often used in a symbolic manner.

LOOK UNDER THE FOLLOWING SUBJECTS IN THE LIBRARY CATALOG

    Heraldry

    Religious Art and Symbolism

    Signs and Symbols

    Symbolism

BROWSE FOR BOOKS ON THE SHELF USING THESE CALL NUMBERS

    133.3 (Symbolism of Divinatory Arts and Objects)

    246 (Use of Art in Christianity, including Symbols)

    291.3 (Religious Symbols)

    704.9 (Iconography)

REFERENCE MATERIALS THAT MAY HELP (BOOKS OR CD-ROMS)

    Baldock, John. *The Elements of Christian Symbolism*. Element Books, 1997.

    Biedermann, Hans. *Dictionary of Symbolism*. Facts on File, 1992.

    Carr-Gomm, Sarah. *The Dictionary of Symbols in Western Art*. Facts on File, 1995.

    Chevalier, Jean, ed. *A Dictionary of Symbols*. Penguin, 1997.

    Fontana, David. *The Secret Language of Symbols: A Visual Key to Symbols and Their Meanings*. Chronicle Books, 1994.

    Liungman, Carl G. *Dictionary of Symbols*. ABC-CLIO, 1991.

PERIODICAL INDEXES

    EBSCO Magazine Article Summaries

    InfoTrac

    Reader's Guide to Periodical Literature

SUGGESTED INTERNET SITES

    http://www.symbols.com (The world's largest online encyclopedia of graphic symbols)

    http://www.heraldica.org/topics/index.html (Heraldry topics and links)

Http://pages.prodigy.com/Christstory/ (Easter symbols and legends)
http://www.cpmgroup.com/symbols.html (Symbol lore)

KEY WORDS FOR PERIODICAL AND ONLINE SEARCHES
Christian Art and Symbolism
Heraldry
Iconography
Signs and Symbols
Symbolism

VIDEO PROGRAMS RELATED TO THIS TOPIC
American Art and Architecture. Alarion, 1991. (Available from Zenger Media.)
Art and Splendor: Michelangelo and The Sistine Chapel. 1994. (Available from Library Video.)
The Empire of Signs. From *American Visions Series*. PBS, 1997.

ORGANIZATION TO CONTACT FOR ADDITIONAL INFORMATION
American College of Heraldry, c/o David R. Wooten, PO Box 1899, Little Rock, AR 72203–1899.

SUGGESTIONS FOR NARROWING THIS TOPIC
Choose a famous cathedral and describe five of its architectural features or artifacts in terms of symbolism.
Describe common pictorial symbols in dream interpretation.
Discuss political cartoons as symbolic representations.

RELATED TOPICS
Communication
History of Writing
Modern Art
Prehistoric Art

This RESEARCH TOPIC GUIDE is intended to help you find information on your topic in a wide variety of sources in this and any other library. Resources, though, are not limited to those described and not all libraries will have the same titles. Please ask a librarian for further guidance.

Puppetry

BACKGROUND

Puppetry has been teaching and delighting people for thousands of years. Puppets were probably first used in religious ceremonies in Ancient Greece, Egypt, and Rome. Today, puppets are used in a variety of ways: to enhance storytime for children; in classrooms to make lessons more interesting; by religious groups to teach Biblical and moral lessons; in hospitals to aid in healing; by children as entertainment; and in theaters as dramatic or comedic productions. There are three kinds of puppets: hand puppets, marionettes, and rod puppets.

LOOK UNDER THE FOLLOWING SUBJECTS IN THE LIBRARY CATALOG

Puppets and Puppet Plays

Shadow Pantomimes and Plays

Theater

BROWSE FOR BOOKS ON THE SHELF USING THESE CALL NUMBERS

791.43 (Puppet Films)

791.5 (Puppetry and Toy Theaters)

792.3 (Pantomime)

REFERENCE MATERIALS THAT MAY HELP (BOOKS OR CD-ROMS)

Buetter, Barbara MacDonald. *Simple Puppets from Everyday Materials.* Sterling, 1998.

Champlin, Connie. *Storytelling with Puppets.* American Library Association, 1997.

Engler, Larry and Carol Fijan. *Making Puppets Come Alive: How to Learn and Teach Hand Puppetry.* Dover, 1997.

Fling, Helen. *Marionettes: How to Make and Work Them.* Dover, 1973.

Lade, Roger. *The Most Excellent Book of How to Be a Puppeteer.* The Millbrook Press, 1996.

World Book's Information Finder. World Book, date varies. (CD-ROM)

PERIODICAL INDEXES

EBSCO Magazine Article Summaries

InfoTrac

Reader's Guide to Periodical Literature

SUGGESTED INTERNET SITES

http://www.sagecraft.com/puppetry (The Puppet home page)

http://www.puppeteers.org (The Puppeteers of America)

http://www.puppet.org/ (Center for Puppetry Arts)

http://www.henson.com (The Jim Henson Company web site)

KEY WORDS FOR PERIODICAL AND ONLINE SEARCHES

Hand Puppets
Puppet Making
Puppet Theater
Puppetry and Marionettes

VIDEO PROGRAMS RELATED TO THIS TOPIC

Basic Puppetry Techniques. Baker and Taylor Video, 1992.
The Muppets Take Manhattan. CBS/FOX, 1985.
The Punch and Judy Man. MacConkey Productions/Warne-Pathe, 1962.

ORGANIZATIONS TO CONTACT FOR ADDITIONAL INFORMATION

Fellowship of Christian Puppeteers, FCP Mail Center, P.O. Box 423, Windham, ME 04062.
Puppeteers of America, c/o Gayle G. Schluta, #5 Cricklewood Path, Pasadena, CA 91107–1002.

SUGGESTIONS FOR NARROWING THIS TOPIC

Describe five different types of puppets and their histories and/or uses.
Explain the fundamentals of marionettes: both building them and using them.
Working with three to five other students, write a puppet play; make your own puppets, stage and scenery; and perform the play for your class.

RELATED TOPICS

Animation
Kites
Magic
Reader's Theater

This RESEARCH TOPIC GUIDE is intended to help you find information on your topic in a wide variety of sources in this and any other library. Resources, though, are not limited to those described and not all libraries will have the same titles. Please ask a librarian for further guidance.

Reading Codes for the Blind

BACKGROUND

Attempts at establishing reading codes for the blind began as early as 1771, when Valentin Hauy conceived the possibility of embossed letters for the blind. Louis Braille, born in 1809 and blinded at the age of three, invented the raised dot alphabet, Braille, now used throughout the world.

LOOK UNDER THE FOLLOWING SUBJECTS IN THE LIBRARY CATALOG

Blind

Blind—Books and Reading

Large Print Books

Talking Books

BROWSE FOR BOOKS ON THE SHELF USING THESE CALL NUMBERS

011.63 (Bibliographies of Books for Handicapped Users)

027.6 (Libraries for Special Groups, such as Persons with Disabilities)

411 (Writing Systems, including Braille)

686.2 (Printing, Typesetting)

REFERENCE MATERIALS THAT MAY HELP (BOOKS OR CD-ROMS)

Espinala. *Solutions Access Technologies for People Who Are Blind*. National Braille Press, 1992.

Hawking, Stephen and the Alliance for Technology Access. *Computer Resources for People with Disabilities: A Guide to Exploring Today's Assistive Technology*. Hunter House, 1996.

McNulty, Tom and Dawn M. Suvino. *Access to Information: Materials, Technologies, and Services for Print-Impaired Readers*. American Library Association, 1993.

Rex, Evelyn J., et al. *Foundations of Braille Literacy*. American Foundation for the Blind, 1994.

Sardengna, Jill and T. Otis Paul. *The Encyclopedia of Blindness and Visual Impairment*. Facts on File, 1991.

PERIODICAL INDEXES

EBSCO Magazine Article Summaries

InfoTrac

Reader's Guide to Periodical Literature

SUGGESTED INTERNET SITES

http://www.nyise.org/blind/barbier.htm (The History of Reading Codes for the Blind) http://www.igc.apc.org/afb/index.html (The American Foundation for the Blind web site)

http://www.shodor.org/braille (BRL: Braille through Remote Learning)

http://www.acb.org/ (American Council of the Blind web site)

KEY WORDS FOR PERIODICAL AND ONLINE SEARCHES

Blind

Blindness

Printing and Writing Systems

Visually Handicapped

VIDEO PROGRAMS RELATED TO THIS TOPIC

Braille Institute Insight Series. (Available from Library Video.)

Dogs: The Ultimate Guide. Discovery Channel. (Available from Library Video.)

Helen Keller (American Women of Achievement Series). Schlessinger, 1995.

ORGANIZATIONS TO CONTACT FOR ADDITIONAL INFORMATION

American Council of the Blind, 1155 15th Street, NW, Suite 720, Washington, DC, 20005. Phone: 202–467–5081, Fax: 202–467–5085.

Lutheran Braille Workers, Inc., 13471 California Street, PO Box 5000, Yucaipa, CA 92399. Phone: 909–795–8977, Fax: 909–795–8970.

SUGGESTIONS FOR NARROWING THIS TOPIC

Discuss the national Agenda for the Education of Children and Youths with Visual Impairments including Those with Multiple Disabilities.

Discuss and describe various types of Braille access technology available today.

Research the history of reading codes for the blind.

RELATED TOPICS

Eye Diseases and Conditions

Guide Dogs

Hearing Impaired

Helen Keller

This RESEARCH TOPIC GUIDE is intended to help you find information on your topic in a wide variety of sources in this and any other library. Resources, though, are not limited to those described and not all libraries will have the same titles. Please ask a librarian for further guidance.

Renaissance Art

BACKGROUND

The Renaissance is a time period in history that began around A.D. 1300 and lasted for approximately 300 years. It was a rich period of development that began in Italy and spread throughout Europe at the end of the Middle Ages, marking the point of departure from the medieval to the modern world.

LOOK UNDER THE FOLLOWING SUBJECTS IN THE LIBRARY CATALOG

> Art—History
>
> Renaissance
>
> Renaissance Architecture
>
> Renaissance Art

Also search under names of particular artists, such as Durer, Albrecht or da Vinci, Leonardo.

BROWSE FOR BOOKS ON THE SHELF USING THESE CALL NUMBERS

> 709.02 (Art, including Renaissance Art)
>
> 724 (Architecture, including Renaissance Architecture)
>
> 734 (Sculpture, including Renaissance Sculpture)

REFERENCE MATERIALS THAT MAY HELP (BOOKS OR CD-ROMS)

> Corrain, Lucia. *The Art of the Renaissance*. Peter Bedrick Books, 1997.
>
> Earls, Irene. *Renaissance Art: A Topical Dictionary*. Greenwood, 1987.
>
> Letts, Rosa Maria. *The Renaissance*. Cambridge University Press, 1992.
>
> *The Renaissance*. Clearvue/eav, 1994. (CD-ROM)
>
> *Renaissance Master I and II*. TDC Interactive Technology, 1992. (CD-ROM)
>
> Tansey, Richard, et al. *Gardner's Art through the Ages: Renaissance and Modern Art*. Harcourt Brace Children's Books, 1995.

PERIODICAL INDEXES

> *EBSCO Magazine Article Summaries*
>
> Index to *History Today* Magazine
>
> *InfoTrac*
>
> *Reader's Guide to Periodical Literature*

SUGGESTED INTERNET SITES

> http://www.nyu.edu/gsas/dept/history/internet/geograph/europe/medieval/art.html (Medieval and Renaissance Art, Architecture and Music)
>
> http://web.uvic.ca/hrd/UAP/renaiold.htm (Links to resources relating to the art and culture of the Italian Renaissance)

http://witcombe.bcpw.sbc.edu/ARTHLinks2.html (Art history resources on
the web)

http://www.harbrace.com/art/gardner/RenBar.html (Gateway to Art History)

KEY WORDS FOR PERIODICAL AND ONLINE SEARCHES

Art, Renaissance

Artists

Fifteenth-Sixteenth Century Art

Renaissance Art

Also search under names of individual artists.

VIDEO PROGRAMS RELATED TO THIS TOPIC

Art of the Western World: Set II. WNET/New York for the Annenberg/CPB
Project, 1989.

Exploring the Renaissance. United Learning, 1994.

The Renaissance. Coronet, 1978.

ORGANIZATIONS TO CONTACT FOR ADDITIONAL
INFORMATION

Center for Medieval and Renaissance Studies, The Ohio State University,
256 Cunz Hall, 1841 Millikin Road, Columbus, OH 43210.

South Central Renaissance Conference, c/o Liana De Girolami Cheney,
President, Department of Art History, University of Massachusetts-
Lowell, 112 Charles Street, Boston, MA 02114. Fax: 617–557–2962.

SUGGESTIONS FOR NARROWING THIS TOPIC

Discuss the effects of the Renaissance upon art.

Discuss the roles women played in the creative processes of Renaissance culture.

Choose an artist, male or female, of the Renaissance period and discuss
his/her life major works.

RELATED TOPICS

Everyday Life during the Renaissance in a Major European Country Such as
England, France, or Italy

Renaissance Music

Renaissance Science

This RESEARCH TOPIC GUIDE is intended to help you find information on your topic in a
wide variety of sources in this and any other library. Resources, though, are not limited to
those described and not all libraries will have the same titles. Please ask a librarian for further
guidance.

Rock and Roll, History of

BACKGROUND

Rock and roll, or popular music, grew out of ragtime and the blues to become the phenomenon as it is now known. Popular especially with young people, rock musicians often write lyrics that address the problems and sentiments of the young or the social issues of the times. The strong beat, sometimes outrageous costumes of the performers, and the special effects used during stage performances are especially appealing to young people.

LOOK UNDER THE FOLLOWING SUBJECTS IN THE LIBRARY CATALOG

> Dance Music
> Electronic Musical Instruments
> Music
> Popular Music
> Rock Music

Also search under the names of individual musicians or music groups.

BROWSE FOR BOOKS ON THE SHELF USING THESE CALL NUMBERS

> 781.63 (Popular Music)
> 781.66 (Rock 'n' Roll)
> 782.42166 (Rock 'n' Roll Songs)

REFERENCE MATERIALS THAT MAY HELP (BOOKS OR CD-ROMS)

> *Apple Pie Music*. Queue, 1994. (CD-ROM)
> *Contemporary Musicians*. Gale Research, 1991. (Multivolume)
> Covach, John Rudolph and Graeme M. Boone, eds. *Understanding Rock: Essays in Musical Analysis*. Oxford University Press, 1997.
> DuNoyer, Paul, ed. *The Story of Rock 'n' Roll: The Year-by-Year Illustrated Chronicle*. Macmillan Library Reference, 1995.
> *Parents Aren't Supposed to Like It: People and Trends in Popular Music*. U.X.L., 1997. (3 volumes)
> *Popular Music*. Gale Research, 1995. (Multivolume)

PERIODICAL INDEXES

> *EBSCO Magazine Article Summaries*
> *InfoTrac*
> *Reader's Guide to Periodical Literature*

SUGGESTED INTERNET SITES

> http://www.music.indiana.edu/som/courses/rock/index.html (Indiana University: History of Rock & Roll and other non-major courses)

http://www.rockhall.com/ (Rock and Roll Hall of Fame web site)

http://www.music.warnerbros.com/rocknroll/ (The History of Rock 'n' Roll web page from Warner Brothers)

http://www.oldiesmusic.com/open.htm (Oldies Music web site)

KEY WORDS FOR PERIODICAL AND ONLINE SEARCHES

Electronic Musical Instruments

Music

Popular Music

Rock Music

Also search using the names of individual musicians and/or groups.

VIDEO PROGRAMS RELATED TO THIS TOPIC

The History of Rock 'n' Roll Series (10 volume set). Time-Life, 1995. (Available from Zenger Media.)

Rock 'n' Roll Collection: Dick Clark's Golden Greats (4 volume set). 1993. (Available from Zenger Media.)

ORGANIZATIONS TO CONTACT FOR ADDITIONAL INFORMATION

Rock Record Collectors Association, 126 Martindale Avenue, Oakville, Ontario, Canada, L6H 4G7.

World Rock 'n' Roll Confederation, Schuetzenstr.8, 80335 Munich, Germany. Info@WITC.org; http://www.wrrc.org/

SUGGESTIONS FOR NARROWING THIS TOPIC

Discuss the development and evolution of the technology used in the production of rock music.

Discuss the influence that rock music has had on American culture. Provide specific examples.

Select a music group and discuss the history of that group's evolution in rock music.

RELATED TOPICS

Bluegrass Music

Gospel Music

Jazz

Rap

This RESEARCH TOPIC GUIDE is intended to help you find information on your topic in a wide variety of sources in this and any other library. Resources, though, are not limited to those described and not all libraries will have the same titles. Please ask a librarian for further guidance.

Utopias

BACKGROUND

A utopia is an ideal community or place where everything is perfect. Many writers have written of an ideal society; likewise, many men and women have dreamed of and even tried to create a utopia in the form of a religious group such as the Shakers or a collective settlement, often referred to as a commune.

LOOK UNDER THE FOLLOWING SUBJECTS IN THE LIBRARY CATALOG

Collective Settlements

Communal Living

Ideal States

Utopias

BROWSE FOR BOOKS ON THE SHELF USING THESE CALL NUMBERS

289 (Alternative Religious Denominations and Sects)

321 (Systems of Governments and States—Utopias)

335 (Socialism and Related Systems—Utopian Systems)

397.77 (Self-Contained Communities: Communes)

REFERENCE MATERIALS THAT MAY HELP (BOOKS OR CD-ROMS)

Fogarty, Robert S. *All Things New: American Communes and Utopian Movements, 1860–1914*. University of Chicago Press, 1990.

Gay, Kathlyn. *Communes and Cults*. Twenty-First Century Books, 1997.

Hollis, Daniel W., III. *The ABC-CLIO World History Companion to Utopian Movements*. ABC-CLIO, 1997.

Nordhoff, Charles and Robert S. Fogarty. *American Utopias*. Berkshire House, 1993.

Snodgrass, Mary Ellen. *Encyclopedia of Utopian Literature*. ABC-CLIO, 1995.

Stockwell, Foster. *Encyclopedia of American Communes, 1663–1963*. McFarland, 1998.

PERIODICAL INDEXES

EBSCO Magazine Article Summaries

InfoTrac

Reader's Guide to Periodical Literature

SUGGESTED INTERNET SITES

http://www.plattsburgh.edu/legacy/utopia_www_resources.html (Resources on alternative and utopian communities)

http://www.ic.org/ (Intentional Communities web site)

KEY WORDS FOR PERIODICAL AND ONLINE SEARCHES

Collective Settlements

Cults

Kibbutzism

Utopias

Also search under names of specific groups, such as Amish, Shakers, New Harmony (Indiana).

VIDEO PROGRAMS RELATED TO THIS TOPIC

The Amish. Schlessinger Media, 1993.

Lost Horizon. 1997. (Available from Filmic Archives.)

The Shakers: Hands to Work, Hearts to God. 1989. (Available from Library Video.)

ORGANIZATIONS TO CONTACT FOR ADDITIONAL INFORMATION

The Fellowship for Intentional Community, Route 1, Box 155, Rutledge, MO 63563.

Society for Utopian Studies, c/o Lyman Tower Sargent, Department of Political Science, University of Missouri-St. Louis, St. Louis, MO 63121–4499.

SUGGESTIONS FOR NARROWING THIS TOPIC

Describe how you would create a utopian society.

Describe life in a Shaker village. What elements of a utopian society existed?

Research and report on why many people who question our society's values choose to live in an "intentional community."

RELATED TOPICS

Communism

Socialism

This RESEARCH TOPIC GUIDE is intended to help you find information on your topic in a wide variety of sources in this and any other library. Resources, though, are not limited to those described and not all libraries will have the same titles. Please ask a librarian for further guidance.

William Shakespeare, Life and Times

BACKGROUND

William Shakespeare (1564–1616), English playwright and poet, is probably the world's most famous writer. During his career he wrote 37 plays, two narrative poems, a short poem, and 154 sonnets. He helped found the Globe Theatre, which was one of the largest theaters in the London area, in the suburb of Southwark in 1599. The huge success of his works has not been without controversy: through the ages the debate continues as to whether Shakespeare was the actual author of the works attributed to him.

LOOK UNDER THE FOLLOWING SUBJECTS IN THE LIBRARY CATALOG

Globe Theatre (Southwark, England)

Great Britain—History—16th Century

Shakespeare, William

BROWSE FOR BOOKS ON THE SHELF USING THESE CALL NUMBERS

792 (Theater)

822.3 (Shakespeare)

942 (English History)

REFERENCE MATERIALS THAT MAY HELP (BOOKS OR CD-ROMS)

Andrews, John F. *William Shakespeare: His World, His Work, His Influence*. Scribner, 1985.

Boyce, Charles and David White. *Shakespeare A to Z: The Essential Reference to His Plays, His Poems, His Life and Times, and More*. Facts on File, 1990.

Exploring Shakespeare. Gale, 1997. (CD-ROM)

Jones, Jeanne. *Family Life in Shakespeare's England: Stratford-Upon-Avon 1570–1630*. Alan Sutton, 1997.

Laroque, François. *The Age of Shakespeare*. Harry N. Abrams, 1993.

Shakespeare for Students. Gale Research, 1992.

Shakespeare's Life and Times. Intellimation, 1994. (CD-ROM)

PERIODICAL INDEXES

EBSCO Magazine Article Summaries

Index to *History Today* Magazine

InfoTrac

Reader's Guide to Periodical Literature

SUGGESTED INTERNET SITES

http://www.stratford-upon-avon.co.uk/soawshst.htm (William Shakespeare of Stratford-upon-Avon: Brief history, times, and references) http://www.Shakespeare-oxford.com (Shakespeare Oxford Society home page)

http://www.Shakespearemag.com (Shakespeare Magazine: A Shakespeare teaching resource)

http://www.folger.edu (Folger Shakespeare Library)

KEY WORDS FOR PERIODICAL AND ONLINE SEARCHES

English Literature

Globe Theatre (London, England)

Great Britain—History—Elizabethan Period, 1485–1603

Shakespeare, William, 1564–1616

VIDEO PROGRAMS RELATED TO THIS TOPIC

Shakespeare: The Man and His Times. Clearvue/eav, 1991.

William Shakespeare: Life of Drama. A & E TV Networks, 1996.

World of William Shakespeare: The Time Is Out of Joint. National Geographic Society, 1978.

ORGANIZATIONS TO CONTACT FOR ADDITIONAL INFORMATION

Horatio Society, c/o Randall Sherman, 99 Cedro Avenue, San Francisco, CA 94127. newven@best.com

Shakespeare Authorship Roundtable, PO Box 1887, Santa Monica, CA 90406.

Shakespeare Oxford Society, PO Box 263, Somerville, MA 02143. Phone: 617–628–3411, Fax: 617–628–4258. everreader@aol.com

SUGGESTIONS FOR NARROWING THIS TOPIC

Discuss the debate over the authorship of Shakespeare's plays.

Discuss the relevancy in our modern society of one of Shakespeare's plays (*Romeo and Juliet, Hamlet, Julius Caesar*, for example).

Prepare an annotated Shakespearean timeline illustrating the key events of Shakespeare's life and works.

RELATED TOPICS

Elizabeth I

Everyday Life in Elizabethan England

History of the Globe Theatre

Science and Medicine in Elizabethan times

This RESEARCH TOPIC GUIDE is intended to help you find information on your topic in a wide variety of sources in this and any other library. Resources, though, are not limited to those described and not all libraries will have the same titles. Please ask a librarian for further guidance.

II

Math, Science, and Technology

Air Pollution

BACKGROUND

Air pollution is a major worldwide economic and health problem. Some of the causes of air pollution include automobile emissions, industry, fuel combustion for heating, and the burning of solid wastes. Air pollution can occur both outdoors and indoors.

LOOK UNDER THE FOLLOWING SUBJECTS IN THE LIBRARY CATALOG

> Air Pollution
> Environment
> Ozone Layer
> Pollution

BROWSE FOR BOOKS ON THE SHELF USING THESE CALL NUMBERS

> 304.2 (Human Ecology)
> 333.7 (Environmental Protection)
> 363.73 (Pollution)
> 628.5 (Industrial Pollution)

REFERENCE MATERIALS THAT MAY HELP (BOOKS OR CD-ROMS)

> *Air: The Nature of Atmosphere and the Climate*. Facts on File, 1992.
> Ashworth, William. *The Encyclopedia of Environmental Studies*. Facts on File, 1991.
> Cunningham, William P., et al., eds. *Environmental Encyclopedia*. Gale, 1997.
> *Land and Air: The Environment*. Mentorom, 1995. (CD-ROM)
> Miller, E. Willard and Ruby M. Miller. *Environmental Hazards: Air Pollution*. ABC-CLIO, 1989.
> Newton, David E. *The Ozone Dilemma*. ABC-CLIO, 1995.

PERIODICAL INDEXES

> *EBSCO Magazine Article Summaries*
> *InfoTrac*
> *Reader's Guide to Periodical Literature*

SUGGESTED INTERNET SITES

> http://www-wilson.ucsd.edu/education/airpollution/airpollution.html (*Air Pollution* from the World of Physical Chemistry)
> http://www.epa.gov (U.S. Environmental Protection Agency online)

http://www.epa.ohio.gov/dapc/page/other.html (Ohio EPA Division of Air Pollution Control: General information and links to other air pollution-related web sites)

http://www.envirolink.org/ (Environlink: The Online Environmental Community)

KEY WORDS FOR PERIODICAL AND ONLINE SEARCHES

Air Pollution

Greenhouse Effect, Atmospheric

Indoor Air Pollution

Smog

VIDEO PROGRAMS RELATED TO THIS TOPIC

Clean Air. Schlessinger, 1993.

Crisis in the Atmosphere: The Infinite Voyage. National Academy of Sciences, 1989.

Ozone Layer. Schlessinger, 1993.

ORGANIZATIONS TO CONTACT FOR ADDITIONAL INFORMATION

Center for Environmental Information, 99 Court Street, Rochester, NY 14604. Phone: 716–546–3796.

Environmental Defense Fund, 257 Park Avenue, South, New York, NY 10010. Phone: 212–505–2100.

Friends of the Earth, 218 D Street, SE, Washington, DC 20003.

SUGGESTIONS FOR NARROWING THIS TOPIC

Create an educational brochure which describes various causes of air pollution and offers solutions.

Discuss the controversy over second-hand cigarette smoke.

Discuss laws and legislation to control air pollution.

RELATED TOPICS

Acid Rain

Global Warming

Ozone Layer

Sick Building Syndrome

This RESEARCH TOPIC GUIDE is intended to help you find information on your topic in a wide variety of sources in this and any other library. Resources, though, are not limited to those described and not all libraries will have the same titles. Please ask a librarian for further guidance.

Bacteria

BACKGROUND

Bacteria are simple one-cell organisms that exist almost everywhere, including in the human body. There are both harmful and harmless bacteria. Many bacteria play vital roles in nature including the decomposition of dead organisms. There are some bacteria that cause diseases in humans, other animals, and plants.

LOOK UNDER THE FOLLOWING SUBJECTS IN THE LIBRARY CATALOG

Bacteria
Bacteriology
Germ Theory of Disease
Microorganisms

BROWSE FOR BOOKS ON THE SHELF USING THESE CALL NUMBERS

576 (Microbiology)
589.9 (Bacteria; Bacteriology)
616.9 (Communicable Diseases)

REFERENCE MATERIALS THAT MAY HELP (BOOKS OR CD-ROMS)

Facklam, Howard and Margery Facklam. *Bacteria*. Twenty-First Century Books, 1995.
Health Quest. Entrex Software, 1997. (CD-ROM)
Human Health. Cambridge Educational, 1997. (CD-ROM)
Lim, Daniel. *Introduction to Microbiology*. Contemporary Publishing Company of Raleigh, 1995.
Marsh, Carole. *Hot Zones: Disease, Epidemics, Viruses and Bacteria*. Gallopade Publishing Group, 1998.
Silverstein, Alvin, et al. *Monerans and Protists*. Twenty-First Century Books, 1996.

PERIODICAL INDEXES

EBSCO Magazine Article Summaries
InfoTrac
Reader's Guide to Periodical Literature

SUGGESTED INTERNET SITES

http://vm.cfsan.fda.gov/~mow/bactoc.html (Food and Drug Administration Foodborne Pathogenic Microorganisms and Natural Toxins) http://www.sciam.com/explorations/072197bacteria/mirsky.html (*Home, Bacteria-Ridden Home* from Scientific American Explorations)

http://jb.asm.org (*Journal of Bacteriology* Online)

KEY WORDS FOR PERIODICAL AND ONLINE SEARCHES

Bacteria

Bacterial Diseases

Bacteriology

Microorganisms

VIDEO PROGRAMS RELATED TO THIS TOPIC

Bacteria. National Geographic, 1998.

Bacteria: Invisible Friends & Foes. Human Relations Media, 1994.

Simple Organisms: Bacteria. Coronet.

ORGANIZATION TO CONTACT FOR ADDITIONAL INFORMATION

American Society for Microbiology, 1325 Massachusettes Avenue, Washington, DC 20005. Phone: 202–737–3600.

SUGGESTIONS FOR NARROWING THIS TOPIC

Compare bacteria and viruses.

Discuss Louis Pasteur's contributions to the field of bacteriology.

Discuss three kinds of harmful bacteria and the diseases they cause in humans.

RELATED TOPICS

Food Safety

Fungi

Parasites

Viruses

This RESEARCH TOPIC GUIDE is intended to help you find information on your topic in a wide variety of sources in this and any other library. Resources, though, are not limited to those described and not all libraries will have the same titles. Please ask a librarian for further guidance.

Comets

BACKGROUND

A comet is an orbital object in space made up of frozen gases and water mixed with dust particles. Most comets cannot be seen with the naked eye; those that can usually generate a lot of excitement from observers, as they can be an awesome sight. Falley's Comet, with its appearance approximately every 77 years, is probably the most famous of comets.

LOOK UNDER THE FOLLOWING SUBJECTS IN THE LIBRARY CATALOG

Astronomy

Comets

Solar System

Also search under names of specific comets, such as Halley's comet.

BROWSE FOR BOOKS ON THE SHELF USING THIS CALL NUMBER

523.6 (Comets)

REFERENCE MATERIALS THAT MAY HELP (BOOKS OR CD-ROMS)

Astronomy. World Book, 1997.

Astronomy and Space: From the Big Bang to the Big Crunch. Gale, 1997.

Brandt, John C. and Robert D. Chapman. *Rendezvous in Space: The Science of Comets*. W. H. Freeman, 1992.

DISCovering Science. Gale, 1997. (CD-ROM)

Eyewitness Encyclopedia of Space and the Universe. DK Multimedia, 1996. (CD-ROM)

Marsh, Carole and Arthur R. Upgren. *Asteroids, Comets, and Meteors*. Twenty-First Century Books, 1996.

PERIODICAL INDEXES

EBSCO Magazine Article Summaries

InfoTrac

Reader's Guide to Periodical Literature

SUGGESTED INTERNET SITES

http://www.challenger.org/ (Challenger Center Online)

http://smallcomets.physics.uiowa.edu/ (Small Comets: Facts, news, and links about small comets)

http://cfa-www.harvard.edu/iau/special/EdgarWilson.html (What to do if you discover a comet) http://www.cometwatch.com/ (The Purkett Observatory web page)

KEY WORDS FOR PERIODICAL AND ONLINE SEARCHES

Asteroids

Astronomy

Comets

Meteors

Solar System

Also search under names of specific comets, such as Halley's Comet.

VIDEO PROGRAMS RELATED TO THIS TOPIC

The Astronomers Series (6-video set). PBS, 1991.

Comets, Meteors and Asteroids. Coronet, 1986.

Exploring Our Solar System. 1995. (Available from Library Video.)

ORGANIZATION TO CONTACT FOR ADDITIONAL INFORMATION

NASA, Education Division, c/o Frank C. Owens, NASA Headquarters, Washington, DC 20546–0001. Phone: 202–358–1110.

SUGGESTIONS FOR NARROWING THIS TOPIC

Discuss one of the following comets, including its discovery, history, recurrences, and composition: Halley, Hyakutake, Hale-Bopp.

Explain how you would know if you had discovered a "new" comet and what you should do to confirm the discovery.

Explain the differences between a comet and a meteor.

RELATED TOPICS

Constellations

Planets

Space Flight

Space Stations

This RESEARCH TOPIC GUIDE is intended to help you find information on your topic in a wide variety of sources in this and any other library. Resources, though, are not limited to those described and not all libraries will have the same titles. Please ask a librarian for further guidance.

Computers, Development and History of

BACKGROUND

The first reliable analog computer was developed by Vannevar Bush in 1930. Early computers were enormous and were first used to solve differential equations. The development of the microprocessor in the 1970's was a major breakthrough, which eventually allowed the production of the relatively inexpensive, compact computers used today.

LOOK UNDER THE FOLLOWING SUBJECTS IN THE LIBRARY CATALOG

> Computer Industry
> Computers
> Computers and Civilization
> Microcomputers

BROWSE FOR BOOKS ON THE SHELF USING THESE CALL NUMBERS

> 004 (Computer Science)
> 303.48 (Computers and Society)
> 338.4 (Computer Industry)

REFERENCE MATERIALS THAT MAY HELP (BOOKS OR CD-ROMS)

> Campbell-Kelly, Martin and William Aspray. *Computer: A History of the Information Machine*. HarperCollins, 1997.
> Ceruzzi, Paul E. *The Information Revolution*. ABC-CLIO, 1997.
> *Development of Technology*. Queue. (CD-ROM)
> *Macmillan Encyclopedia of Computers*. Macmillan, 1992.
> Shurkin, Joel N. *Engines of the Mind: The Evolution of the Computer from Mainframes to Microprocessors*. W. W. Norton, 1996.
> Spencer, Donald D. *The Timetable of Computers: A Chronology of the Most Important People and Events in the History of Computers*. Camelot, 1997.

SUGGESTED INTERNET SITES

> http://www.cise.nsf.gov/ (National Science Foundation: Directorate for Computer and Information Science and Engineering web page)
> http://www.islandnet.com/~kpolsson/comphist.htm (Chronology of events in the history of microcomputers)

http://www.cs.uregina.ca/~bayko/cpu.html (Great microprocessors of the
past and present, and links to other web sites)
http://www.galactic.co.uk/iainf/computers.html (Historic computers)

KEY WORDS FOR PERIODICAL AND ONLINE SEARCHES

Artificial Intelligence
Computer Industry
Computers
Microcomputers
Supercomputers

VIDEO PROGRAMS RELATED TO THIS TOPIC

Artificial Intelligence. Pangea, 1995.
From Information to Wisdom? Smithsonian.
Inventing the Future. Scientific American Frontiers, 1996.

ORGANIZATIONS TO CONTACT FOR ADDITIONAL INFORMATION

Computer History Association of California, 4159-C El Camino Way, Palo
Alto, CA 94306–4010.
The Computer Museum History Center, Building T-12A, Moffett Federal
Airfield, Mountain View, CA 94035–1000.
Historical Computer Society, 2962 Park Street #1, Jacksonville, FL 32205.

SUGGESTIONS FOR NARROWING THIS TOPIC

Create an annotated timeline denoting important landmarks in computer development.
Discuss how computers have transformed American homes, schools, and the
workplace.
Research the development of computers.

RELATED TOPICS

Artificial Intelligence
Computer Hackers
Electronic Calculator History
Internet or World Wide Web History
Robotics
Virtual Reality

This RESEARCH TOPIC GUIDE is intended to help you find information on your topic in a
wide variety of sources in this and any other library. Resources, though, are not limited to
those described and not all libraries will have the same titles. Please ask a librarian for further
guidance.

Diseases

BACKGROUND

Disease is a disorder of the body or mind. Infectious diseases are caused by micro-organisms such as bacteria or viruses. All other diseases are classed as noninfectious diseases and are caused by poor diet, birth defects, environmental hazards, stress, or simply the breakdown of tissues and organs as a result of aging.

LOOK UNDER THE FOLLOWING SUBJECTS IN THE LIBRARY CATALOG

Diseases

Health

Medicine

Also search under names of specific diseases or under body parts with the sub-heading "Diseases" (example: Heart—Diseases).

BROWSE FOR BOOKS ON THE SHELF USING THESE CALL NUMBERS

610 (Medicine)

613 (Disease Prevention)

616–616.99 (Diseases)

REFERENCE MATERIALS THAT MAY HELP (BOOKS OR CD-ROMS)

Diseases (8 volumes). Grolier Educational, 1997.

Diseases (Nurse's Ready Reference Series). Springhouse, 1991.

Human Health. Cambridge Educational, 1997. (CD-ROM)

Mayo Clinic Family Health. IVI, 1995. (CD-ROM)

Professional Guide to Diseases. Springhouse, 1998.

The World Book Rush-Presbyterian-St. Luke's Medical Center Medical Encyclopedia: Your Guide to Good Health. World Book, 1998.

PERIODICAL INDEXES

EBSCO Magazine Article Summaries

InfoTrac

Reader's Guide to Periodical Literature

TOM Health and Science

SUGGESTED INTERNET SITES

http://chid.nih.gov/ (Combined health information database online: National Institute of Health)

http://www.cdc.gov/ (Home page of Centers for Disease Control and Prevention) http://www.who.int/ (Home page of the World Health Organization)

http://www.healthfinder.org/default.htm (Healthfinder: A gateway consumer health and human service)

KEY WORDS FOR PERIODICAL AND ONLINE SEARCHES

Diseases

Medicine

Also search under the names of specific diseases, or under the names of body parts with the subheading "Diseases."

VIDEO PROGRAMS RELATED TO THIS TOPIC

Health Risk Appraisal. HRM Software.

The Schlessinger Teen Health Video Series (15 videos). Schlessinger, 1996.

ORGANIZATIONS TO CONTACT FOR ADDITIONAL INFORMATION

Centers for Disease Control and Prevention, 1600 Clifton Road, NE, Atlanta, GA 30333. http://www.cdc.gov

National Institute of Health, Bethesda, MD 20892. http://www.nih.gov

SUGGESTIONS FOR NARROWING THIS TOPIC

Create a poster which informs your target audience of proper disease prevention tactics.

Research a disease, focusing especially on causes, the body part affected, diagnosis, prognosis, symptoms, cures, and preventions.

RELATED TOPICS

Bioethics

Eating Disorders

Health Plan Bill of 1998

Safety

This RESEARCH TOPIC GUIDE is intended to help you find information on your topic in a wide variety of sources in this and any other library. Resources, though, are not limited to those described and not all libraries will have the same titles. Please ask a librarian for further guidance.

Dolphins

BACKGROUND

Dolphins are true mammals that live in water in groups called pods, which include from three to eleven dolphins. There are 32 dolphin species; five live in fresh water and the rest are salt water dwellers. They are found in all oceans and seas of the world.

LOOK UNDER THE FOLLOWING SUBJECTS IN THE LIBRARY CATALOG

Dolphins
Marine Animals
Marine Biology
Whales

BROWSE FOR BOOKS ON THE SHELF USING THESE CALL NUMBERS

551.46 (Oceanography)
599.5 (Cetaceans, that is, dolphins and whales)

REFERENCE MATERIALS THAT MAY HELP (BOOKS OR CD-ROMS)

Bonner, Nigel. *Whales of the World*. Facts on File, 1989.
Encyclopedia of Mammals. Marshall Cavendish, 1997.
Gravelle, Karen. *Animal Societies*. Franklin Watts, 1993.
Harrison, Sir Richard and Michael Bryden, eds. *Whales, Dolphins, and Porpoises*. Facts on File, 1988.
Ocean Life Series. Sumeria, 1993–1997. (6 CD-ROMs)
Whales and Dolphins of the World. Queue. (CD-ROM)

PERIODICAL INDEXES

EBSCO Magazine Article Summaries
InfoTrac
Reader's Guide to Periodical Literature
TOM Health and Science

SUGGESTED INTERNET SITES

http://www.aza.org (American Zoo and Aquarium Associates)
http://www.seaworld.org (Sea World/Busch Gardens Animal Information database)
http://wwwa.com/dolphin (The Wild Dolphin Project)
http://www.dolphinsplus.com/ (Dolphins Plus Online)

KEY WORDS FOR PERIODICAL AND ONLINE SEARCHES

Dolphins
Killer Whales
Marine Biology
Oceanography

VIDEO PROGRAMS RELATED TO THIS TOPIC

Captive Dolphins & Whales: North America/Europe. Discovery Communications, 1992.

Dolphins. PBS, 1995.

Dolphins: Close Encounters. Wolfgang Bayer Production in Association with Thirteen/WNET and Granada Television, 1992.

ORGANIZATIONS TO CONTACT FOR FURTHER INFORMATION

American Zoo & Aquarium Association, 8403 Colesville Road, Suite 710, Silver Spring, MD 20910. Phone: 301–562–0777, Fax: 301–562–0888. www.aza.org/

Dolphins Plus, Inc., PO Box 2728, Key Largo, FL 33037. Phone: 305–451–1993.

Wild Dolphin Project, PO Box 8436, Jupiter, FL 33465. Phone: 561–575–5660.

SUGGESTIONS FOR NARROWING THIS TOPIC

Create an informative poster or video program outlining what people can do to help save dolphins.

Describe the physical characteristics and habitats of three species of dolphins (examples: bottlenose dolphin, humpbacked dolphin, Atlantic spotted dolphin).

Elaborate upon the behavior and social structure of the bottlenose dolphin.

Explain dolphin communication. (See especially http://www.seaworld.org/bottlenose_dolphin/echodol.html)

RELATED TOPICS

Coral Reefs
Fish
Sharks
Walruses

This RESEARCH TOPIC GUIDE is intended to help you find information on your topic in a wide variety of sources in this and any other library. Resources, though, are not limited to those described and not all libraries will have the same titles. Please ask a librarian for further guidance.

El Niño

BACKGROUND

El Niño is a change in the ocean-atmosphere system in the eastern Pacific that contributes to significant weather changes around the world. It is one part of the Southern Oscillation, which is the natural shift of ocean temperatures from year to year; thus, scientists prefer to call the phenomenon of El Niño "ENSO" (the El Nino-Southern Oscillation).

LOOK UNDER THE FOLLOWING SUBJECTS IN THE LIBRARY CATALOG

> Climate
> Meteorology
> Weather
> Weather Forecasting

BROWSE FOR BOOKS ON THE SHELF USING THESE CALL NUMBERS

> 551.5 (Meteorology)
> 551.6 (Climatology and Weather)

REFERENCE MATERIALS THAT MAY HELP (BOOKS OR CD-ROMS)

> Arnold, Caroline. *El Niño: Stormy Weather for People and Wildlife*. Clarion Books, 1998.
> Bigg, Grant R. *The Oceans and Climate*. Cambridge University Press, 1997.
> *The Complete Weather Resource*. U.X.L., 1997.
> *El Niño CD-ROM*. Cdr Software, 1998. (CD-ROM)
> Simons, Paul. *Weird Weather*. Little Brown, 1997.
> *Weather & Climate*. Time-Life Education, 1995.
> *The World's Weather*. Cambridge Educational, 1997. (CD-ROM)

PERIODICAL INDEXES

> *EBSCO Magazine Article Summaries*
> *InfoTrac*
> *Reader's Guide to Periodical Literature*
> *TOM Health and Science*

SUGGESTED INTERNET SITES

> http://darwin.bio.uci.edu/~sustain/ENSO.html (The 1997 El Niño/Southern Oscillation)
> http://www.ogp.noaa.gov/enso/ (El Niño-Southern Oscillation home page)

http://www.sfgate.com/science/pages/1998/el-nino.shtml (El Niño Grande)
http://kids.mtpe.hq.nasa.gov/archive/nino/intro.html (El Niño: An Introduction)

KEY WORDS FOR PERIODICAL AND ONLINE SEARCHES

Climate
El Niño Current
Ocean-Atmosphere Interaction
Southern Oscillation
Weather

VIDEO PROGRAM RELATED TO THIS TOPIC

Oceans and Climate. Coronet.

ORGANIZATIONS TO CONTACT FOR ADDITIONAL INFORMATION

Climate Prediction Center, World Weather Building, 5200 Auth Road, Room 800, Washington, DC 20233. http://www.nnic.noaa.gov/cpc/

National Oceanic and Atmospheric Administration, Office of Public and Constituent Affairs, U.S. Department of Commerce, 14th Street & Constitution Avenue, NW, Room 6013, Washington DC 20230. Phone: 202–482–6090, Fax: 202–482–3154.

SUGGESTIONS FOR NARROWING THIS TOPIC

Discuss the economic impacts of El Niño.
Explain the differences between El Niño and La Niña.
How do scientists predict, forecast, and measure El Niños?
What is an El Niño, and how does one affect the climate?

RELATED TOPICS

Lightning
Meteorology
Seasons
Tornadoes

This RESEARCH TOPIC GUIDE is intended to help you find information on your topic in a wide variety of sources in this and any other library. Resources, though, are not limited to those described and not all libraries will have the same titles. Please ask a librarian for further guidance.

Elements, Chemical

BACKGROUND

Everything on Earth is made up of chemical elements. They are the simplest substances into which ordinary matter may be divided. All other materials are formed by the combination of two or more of the elements.

LOOK UNDER THE FOLLOWING SUBJECTS IN THE LIBRARY CATALOG

Chemical Elements

Periodical Law

Physical Chemistry

Also search under names of individual chemical elements.

BROWSE FOR BOOKS ON THE SHELF USING THESE CALL NUMBERS

541.2 (Periodic Law)

546 (Inorganic Chemistry)

REFERENCE MATERIALS THAT MAY HELP (BOOKS OR CD-ROMS)

DISCovering Science. Gale Research, 1997. (CD-ROM)

Elements (15 volumes). Grolier Educational, 1997.

Interactive Periodic Table. (Available from Library Video.) (CD-ROM)

Krebs, Robert E. *The History and Use of Our Earth's Chemical Elements*. Greenwood, 1997.

Newton, David E. *The Chemical Elements*. Franklin Watts, 1994.

Stwerka, Albert. *A Guide to the Elements*. Oxford University Press, 1996.

PERIODICAL INDEXES

EBSCO Magazine Article Summaries

InfoTrac

Reader's Guide to Periodical Literature

TOM Health and Science

SUGGESTED INTERNET SITES

http://www.webelements.com/index.html (The Periodic Table on the WWW: WebElements)

http://chemlab.pc.maricopa.edu/periodic/periodic.html (The Pictorial Periodic Table)

http://www.ucc.ie/ucc/depts/chem/dolchem/html/elem/elem000.html (The Chemical Elements: details about each)

http://www.nrc.gov/NRC/EDUCATE/REACTOR/02–FISS/part03.html (Elements and Isotopes from the U.S. Nuclear Regulatory Commission)

KEY WORDS FOR PERIODICAL AND ONLINE SEARCHES
Chemical Elements
Chemistry
Periodic Table

VIDEO PROGRAMS RELATED TO THIS TOPIC
Chemical Bonding and Atomic Structure. Coronet.
Elements, Compounds, and Mixtures. Coronet.
The Periodic Table: Reactions and Relationships. Knowledge Unlimited, 1996.

ORGANIZATIONS TO CONTACT FOR ADDITIONAL INFORMATION
American Chemical Society, 1155 16th Street, NW, Washington, DC 20036.
Phone: 202–872–4600.
Chemical Heritage Foundation. http://www.chemheritage.org/

SUGGESTIONS FOR NARROWING THIS TOPIC
Explain the atomic theory of matter.
Relate the history of the development of the periodic table.
Report on a chemical element of your choice. Include in your report the following information: symbol, atomic number, common valence, atomic weight, natural state, common isotopes, characteristics, examples of common compounds, and hazards.

RELATED TOPICS
Chemistry in Everyday Life, Such as in the Kitchen, in the Garden, in the Laundry Room, in the Bathroom
New Materials from Molecules and Atoms

This RESEARCH TOPIC GUIDE is intended to help you find information on your topic in a wide variety of sources in this and any other library. Resources, though, are not limited to those described and not all libraries will have the same titles. Please ask a librarian for further guidance.

Flight

BACKGROUND

For thousands of years before Orville and Wilbur Wright made the first successful powered airplane flight in 1903, man had dreamed about and had made attempts to fly. Some of the first actual manned flights were made in hot air balloons as early as 1783. Later, airships which had engines and propellers, were developed. But, it was the Wright brothers and their planes that jump-started flight as it is known today.

LOOK UNDER THE FOLLOWING SUBJECTS IN THE LIBRARY CATALOG

> Aeronautics
> Airplanes
> Airships
> Flight

BROWSE FOR BOOKS ON THE SHELF USING THIS CALL NUMBER

> 629.13 (Aeronautics)

REFERENCE MATERIALS THAT MAY HELP (BOOKS OR CD-ROMS)

> Baker, David. *Flight and Flying: A Chronology*. Facts on File, 1994.
> Bilstein, Roger E. *Flight in America: From the Wrights to the Astronauts*. Johns Hopkins University Press, 1994.
> Boyne, Walter J. *The Smithsonian Book of Flight*. Smithsonian Books, 1987.
> *History of Aviation*. 1996. (Available from Franklin McNeal.) (CD-ROM)
> Scott, Phil. *The Shoulder of Giants*. Addison-Wesley, 1995.
> *Wright Brothers Collection of Historical Aeronautical Photographs*. Visual Information. 1997. Phone: 303–864–0490. (CD-ROM)

PERIODICAL INDEXES

> *EBSCO Magazine Article Summaries*
> *InfoTrac*
> *Reader's Guide to Periodical Literature*

SUGGESTED INTERNET SITES

> http://www.geocities.com/CapeCanaveral/1998./ (Cyber Flight Deck: History of aviation, simulators, etcetera)
> http://www.helis.com/ (The historical Evolution of Rotary Wing Aircraft: Helicopter History)
> http://www.pbs.org/wgbh/nova/supersonic (NOVA Online: Supersonic Spies: Explore the future of air travel)

KEY WORDS FOR PERIODICAL AND ONLINE SEARCHES

Aeronautics

Aviation—History

Flight

VIDEO PROGRAMS RELATED TO THIS TOPIC

The First Flight. Abrose, 1997.

The Flying Machines. Smithsonian.

Flying the Blimp. PBS/NOVA. (Available from Library Video.)

ORGANIZATION TO CONTACT FOR ADDITIONAL INFORMATION

Women in Aviation International, Morningstar Airport, 3647 S.R. 503, West Alexandria, OH 45381. Phone: 937–839–4647, Fax: 937–839–4645. wai@infinet.com

SUGGESTIONS FOR NARROWING THIS TOPIC

Discuss the Tuskegee Airmen and the contributions they made during World War II.

Research the history of flight.

What does the future hold for air travel?

RELATED TOPICS

Automobiles

Trains and Railroads

Women in Aviation

This RESEARCH TOPIC GUIDE is intended to help you find information on your topic in a wide variety of sources in this and any other library. Resources, though, are not limited to those described and not all libraries will have the same titles. Please ask a librarian for further guidance.

Hormones

BACKGROUND

Hormones are substances secreted in the body via the blood stream by the endocrine glands. Their purpose is to evoke a specific response in other cells of the body. An imbalance of any of the hormones can cause endocrine disease or disorders. Artificial hormones are usually prescribed when an imbalance occurs, but are also used for other reasons, such as anti-aging solutions or growth boosters.

LOOK UNDER THE FOLLOWING SUBJECTS IN THE LIBRARY CATALOG

Endocrine Glands

Endocrinology

Hormones

Also search under names of particular endocrine glands such as "Thyroid," particular body parts affected such as "Kidney," or under particular disorders such as "Diabetes."

BROWSE FOR BOOKS ON THE SHELF USING THESE CALL NUMBERS

574.19 (Biochemistry)

612.4 (Hormones and Endocrine System)

616.4 (Endocrinology)

REFERENCE MATERIALS THAT MAY HELP (BOOKS OR CD-ROMS)

Braem, Thomas. *The Endocrine System*. Bryan Edwards, 1994.

Diseases. Grolier Educational, 1997.

How Your Body Works. Mindscape, 1995. (CD-ROM)

Little, Marjorie and Dale C. Garell. *The Endocrine System: The Healthy Body*. Chelsea House, 1990.

The Ultimate Human Body. Dorling Kindersley, 1996. (CD-ROM)

Young, John K. *Hormones: Molecular Messengers*. Franklin Watts, 1994.

PERIODICAL INDEXES

EBSCO Magazine Article Summaries

InfoTrac

Reader's Guide to Periodical Literature

TOM Health and Science

SUGGESTED INTERNET SITES

http://www.endocrineweb.com/index.html (Endocrine diseases: definitions, overviews, search feature)

http://www.epa.gov/endocrine (Endocrine Disrupters Research Initiative) http://www.healthfinder.org/default.htm (Healthfind: A gateway consumer health and human services information site)

KEY WORDS FOR PERIODICAL AND ONLINE SEARCHES

Endocrine Glands
Endocrine System
Endocrinology
Hormones
Also search under names of particular hormones.

VIDEO PROGRAMS RELATED TO THIS TOPIC

Body Atlas: Glands and Hormones. American Brain Tumor Association, 1997.

Chemistry of Life: Hormones and Endocrine System. Baker and Taylor Video, 1993.

Endocrine System. Louisiana State University Press, 1998.

ORGANIZATION TO CONTACT FOR ADDITIONAL INFORMATION

The Hormone Foundation, 4350 East West Highway, Suite 500, Bethesda, MD 20814–4410. Phone: 1–800–HORMONE, Fax: 301–941–0259.

SUGGESTIONS FOR NARROWING THIS TOPIC

Discuss exposure to environmental chemicals that interact with the endocrine system. (See especially http://www.epa.gov/endocrine)

Discuss the controversy surrounding anti-aging hormone supplements.

Select one of the endocrine glands and provide the following information: location in the human body, function, common disorders, treatment(s) of disorders.

RELATED TOPICS

Athletes and Drugs
Food Additives

This RESEARCH TOPIC GUIDE is intended to help you find information on your topic in a wide variety of sources in this and any other library. Resources, though, are not limited to those described and not all libraries will have the same titles. Please ask a librarian for further guidance.

Invertebrates

BACKGROUND

Invertebrates are animals with no backbones, insects being the most common of the invertebrates. They include animals such as shrimps, crabs, sponges, worms, jellyfishes, snails, and squids. The smallest invertebrates are the protozoans, which are microscopic one-cell animals.

LOOK UNDER THE FOLLOWING SUBJECTS IN THE LIBRARY CATALOG

Insects

Invertebrates

Protozoa

BROWSE FOR BOOKS ON THE SHELF USING THESE CALL NUMBERS

592 (Invertebrates)

593 (Protozoa, Parazoa, Coelenterata, Echinodermata, etcetera)

594 (Mollusks)

595 (Worms, Crustaceans, Arachnids, Progoneata, Insects)

REFERENCE MATERIALS THAT MAY HELP (BOOKS OR CD-ROMS)

Buchsbaum, Ralph, et al. *Animals without Backbones*. University of Chicago Press, 1987.

Invertebrates. National Geographic Society, 1998. (CD-ROM)

Levin, Harold L. *Ancient Invertebrates and Their Living Relatives*. Prentice Hall, 1998.

MacLeod, Beatrice. *Insects and Other Invertebrates*. Gareth Stevens, 1997.

Pennak, Robert William. *Fresh-Water Invertebrates of the United States: Protozoa to Mollusca*. John Wiley & Sons, 1989.

Stidworthy, John. *Simple Animals*. Facts on File, 1990.

PERIODICAL INDEXES

EBSCO Magazine Article Summaries

InfoTrac

Reader's Guide to Periodicals

TOM Health and Science

SUGGESTED INTERNET SITES

http://www.ucmp.berkeley.edu/porifera/porifera.html (Introduction to porifera)

http://www.ufsia.ac.be/Arachnology/Arachnology.html (The arachnology home page: The Arachnological Hub of the World Wide Web)

http://mgfx.com/butterfly/ (The Butterfly web site)

http://www.nmnh.si.edu/departments/invert.html (National Museum of
Natural History Smithsonian Institution: Department of Invertebrate
Zoology)

KEY WORDS FOR PERIODICAL AND ONLINE SEARCHES

Freshwater Invertebrates

Insects

Invertebrates

Also search under names of individual invertebrates.

VIDEO PROGRAMS RELATED TO THIS TOPIC

Insect Life Cycles. Coronet, 1980.

Little Creatures Who Run the World. PBS/NOVA, 1997. (Available from
Time-Life Education.)

Sponges, Coelenterates and Worms. Coronet, 1991.

ORGANIZATIONS TO CONTACT FOR ADDITIONAL INFORMATION

Society for Invertebrate Pathology, 4300 NW 23rd Drive, Suite 78, PO Box
147050, Gainesville, FL 32614–7050. Phone: 1–888–485–1505, Fax:
352–374–5966. sipinfo@gator.net

Young Entomologists' Society, Inc., 1915 Peggy Place, Lansing, MI
48910–2553. http://insects.ummz.lsa.umich.edu/yes/yes.html

SUGGESTIONS FOR NARROWING THIS TOPIC

Create an annotated chart illustrating the life cycle of an invertebrate.

Describe the physical differences between insects and arachnids.

Research an invertebrate of your choice. Include especially its order and
common name, characteristics, habitat, life cycle, behavior, benefits or
harm to humans, natural enemies.

RELATED TOPICS

Animal Behavior

Animal Camouflages

Habitats

This RESEARCH TOPIC GUIDE is intended to help you find information on your topic in a
wide variety of sources in this and any other library. Resources, though, are not limited to
those described and not all libraries will have the same titles. Please ask a librarian for further
guidance.

Lasers

BACKGROUND

A laser is a thin beam of light that is so intense it can cut through dense materials or produce such searing heat that it can burn a hole in a diamond. The word "laser" stands for the process that it uses to produce light: Light Amplification by Stimulated Emission of Radiation.

LOOK UNDER THE FOLLOWING SUBJECTS IN THE LIBRARY CATALOG

Lasers

Light

Also search in particular subjects or fields of endeavor, such as "Lasers in Medicine."

BROWSE FOR BOOKS ON THE SHELF USING THIS CALL NUMBER

621.36 (Lasers)

REFERENCE MATERIALS THAT MAY HELP (BOOKS OR CD-ROMS)

Asimov, Isaac. *How Did We Find Out about Lasers?* Walker & Co., 1990.

Billings, Charlene W. *Lasers: The New Technology of Light.* Facts on File, 1992.

DISCovering Science. Gale Research, 1997. (CD-ROM)

Fox, Mary Virginia. *Lasers.* Marshall Cavendish, 1995.

Harbison, James P. and Robert E. Nahory. *Lasers: Harnessing the Atom's Light.* W. H. Freeman, 1997.

Morgan, Nina. *Lasers.* Raintree/Steck-Vaughn, 1997.

PERIODICAL INDEXES

EBSCO Magazine Article Summaries

InfoTrac

Reader's Guide to Periodical Literature

TOM Health and Science

SUGGESTED INTERNET SITES

http://www.aslms.org/ (American Society for Laser Medicine and Surgery, Inc. home page)

http://www.twi.co.uk/techtran/lasers.html (Make It with Lasers: Focuses on practical aspects of applying lasers to manufacturing tasks)

http://www.oxfordlasers.com (Oxford Lasers home page)

KEY WORDS FOR PERIODICAL AND ONLINE SEARCHES

Laser Fusion

Laser Radar

Laser Spectroscopy

Lasers

Also search under specific types of lasers, such as Blue Lasers, Free Electron Lasers, or X-ray Lasers.

VIDEO PROGRAM RELATED TO THIS TOPIC

The Laser's Edge. PBS, 1995. (Available from Library Video.)

ORGANIZATION TO CONTACT FOR ADDITIONAL INFORMATION

Laser Institute of America, 12424 Research Parkway, Suite 125, Orlando, FL 32826. Phone: 407–380–1553, Fax: 407–380–5588.

SUGGESTIONS FOR NARROWING THIS TOPIC

Discuss everyday applications of lasers in one of the following areas: business, construction, entertainment, industry, law enforcement, medicine, military, or scientific research.

Discuss dangers associated with lasers.

Research the history of lasers.

RELATED TOPICS

Atom

Holography

Light

Optics

This RESEARCH TOPIC GUIDE is intended to help you find information on your topic in a wide variety of sources in this and any other library. Resources, though, are not limited to those described and not all libraries will have the same titles. Please ask a librarian for further guidance.

Nuclear Energy

BACKGROUND

The source of nuclear energy is the atom. It was not until the 20th century that scientists learned to release this energy and put it to use. Because of the great amounts of heat that nuclear energy can create, it can be used to generate steam, which, in turn, generates electricity. There is much controversy surrounding the use of nuclear energy because of its potential to cause great destruction and environmental harm.

LOOK UNDER THE FOLLOWING SUBJECTS IN THE LIBRARY CATALOG

Nuclear Energy

Nuclear Industry

Nuclear Power Plants

Nuclear Reactors

BROWSE FOR BOOKS ON THE SHELF USING THESE CALL NUMBERS

333.792 (Nuclear Energy)

539.7 (Atomic and Nuclear Physics)

621.48 (Nuclear Reactors and Nuclear Power Plants)

REFERENCE MATERIALS THAT MAY HELP (BOOKS OR CD-ROMS)

Daley, Michael J. *Nuclear Power: Promise or Peril?* Lerner, 1997.

DISCovering Science. Gale Research, 1997. (CD-ROM)

Galperin, Anne L. *Nuclear Energy/Nuclear Waste.* Chelsea, 1992.

Henderson, Harry. *Nuclear Physics.* Facts on File, 1998.

Understanding Energy. Cambridge Educational, 1997. (CD-ROM)

PERIODICAL INDEXES

EBSCO Magazine Article Summaries

InfoTrac

Reader's Guide to Periodical Literature

TOM Health and Science

SUGGESTED INTERNET SITES

http://www.ne.doe.gov/ (Nuclear power plants: design, operations, maintenance, engineering)

http://www.nsf.gov/ (Nuclear Free Web—links to articles)

http://www.cannon.net/~gonyeau/nuclear/design.htm (U.S. Department of Energy: Office of Nuclear Energy, Science, and Technology: Overview, current issues, public information, energy facts, links)

http://ecosys.drdr.virginia.edu/sea/nuke.html (National Science Foundation home page)

KEY WORDS FOR PERIODICAL AND ONLINE SEARCHES

Anti-Nuclear Movement
Nuclear Energy
Nuclear Power Plants
Nuclear Reactors
Nuclear Weapons

VIDEO PROGRAMS RELATED TO THIS TOPIC

Nuclear Energy/Nuclear Waste. Schlessinger Media, 1993.
Power for the People. Coronet/MTI Film & Video.

ORGANIZATIONS TO CONTACT FOR ADDITIONAL INFORMATION

American Nuclear Society, 555 N. Kensington Avenue, LaGrange Park, IL 60526. Phone: 708–352–6611, Fax: 708–352–0499.

U.S. Department of Energy, Office of Nuclear Energy, Science, and Technology, 19901 Germantown Road, Germantown, MD 20874–1290. ne-web@hq.doe.gov

SUGGESTIONS FOR NARROWING THIS TOPIC

Create an annotated timetable documenting the development of nuclear weapons from 1920 to the present.

Create a poster which illustrates and labels the key areas and buildings of a nuclear power plant.

Present the pros and cons of the following question: Do the risks of nuclear power outweigh the benefits?

Discuss government regulations and laws regarding nuclear power plants in the United States, and compare them with those of one of the following countries: Canada, France, Japan.

RELATED TOPICS

Alternative Energy Resources
Energy Conservation
Water Power

This RESEARCH TOPIC GUIDE is intended to help you find information on your topic in a wide variety of sources in this and any other library. Resources, though, are not limited to those described and not all libraries will have the same titles. Please ask a librarian for further guidance.

Nutrition

BACKGROUND

Good nutrition is essential for a healthy life. Modern dietary guidelines published by the U.S. Department of Agriculture and the Department of Health and Human Services advise eating a wide variety of foods with plenty of vegetables, fruits, and grains; low in fat, salt, sodium, and sugars; and low alcoholic intake. A Food Guide Pyramid is a guide to daily food choices recommending intake from five different food groups.

LOOK UNDER THE FOLLOW SUBJECTS IN THE LIBRARY CATALOG

Diet
Food
Malnutrition
Nutrition

BROWSE FOR BOOKS ON THE SHELF USING THESE CALL NUMBERS

613.2 (Dietetics, Vitamins)
641.1 (Applied Nutrition)
641.3 (Food)

REFERENCE MATERIALS THAT MAY HELP (BOOKS OR CD-ROMS)

American Medical Association Family Medical Guide. DK Multimedia, 1996. (CD-ROM)

Cheraskin, E., et al. *Diet and Disease.* Keats, 1995.

Duyff, Roberta Larson. *The American Dietetic Association's Complete Food and Nutrition Guide.* Chronimed, 1998.

Ensminger, Audrey H., et al. *The Concise Encyclopedia of Foods and Nutrition.* CRC Press, 1995.

Ronzio, Robert A. *The Encyclopedia of Nutrition and Good Health.* Facts on File, 1997.

Taking Control of Your Health. IVI, 1996. (CD-ROM)

PERIODICAL INDEXES

EBSCO Magazine Article Summaries
InfoTrac
Reader's Guide to Periodical Literature
TOM Health and Science

SUGGESTED INTERNET SITES

http://www.eatright.org/ (American Dietetic Association on the Net) http://dawp.anet.com (Diet analysis web page)

http://www.olen.com/food/ (Fast food facts: Interactive food finder)

http://www.room42.com/nutrition/basal.html (Room 42 Software's basal metabolism calculator)

KEY WORDS FOR PERIODICAL AND ONLINE SEARCHES

Diet

Malnutrition

Nutrition

Vitamins

VIDEO PROGRAMS RELATED TO THIS TOPIC

The Food Guide Pyramid. Cambridge, 1993.

Meal Planning: The Food Pyramid in Action. Learning Seed, 1996.

Nutrition and Diet. Schlessinger Media, 1994.

ORGANIZATIONS TO CONTACT FOR ADDITIONAL INFORMATION

American Dietetic Association, 216 West Jackson Boulevard, Chicago, IL 60606–6005. Phone: 312–899–0040, Fax: 312–899–1979.

International Food Information Council, 1100 Connecticut Avenue, N.W., Suite 430, Washington, DC 20036. http:/foodinfo@ific.health.org

SUGGESTIONS FOR NARROWING THIS TOPIC

Discuss the latest dietary guidelines published by the U.S. Department of Agriculture and Health and Human Services.

Discuss the role of exercise and nutrition in health and disease control.

Keep a chart of everything you eat for one week, then go to the Diet Analysis Web Page to analyze your diet: http://dawp.@anet.com

RELATED TOPICS

Allergies

Eating Disorders

Fitness

Vegetarianism

This RESEARCH TOPIC GUIDE is intended to help you find information on your topic in a wide variety of sources in this and any other library. Resources, though, are not limited to those described and not all libraries will have the same titles. Please ask a librarian for further guidance.

Parasites

BACKGROUND

Animals may become infected by other organisms called parasites. A wide variety of organisms can be parasitic, including roundworms, flatworms, segmented worms, and protozoa. Control of parasites can be by chemotherapy, immunization, sanitation, or separation of the host from sources of infection.

LOOK UNDER THE FOLLOWING SUBJECTS IN THE LIBRARY CATALOG

Parasites

Pests

Ticks

Also search under names of particular kinds of parasites, such as roundworms, tapeworms, or flukes.

BROWSE FOR BOOKS ON THE SHELF USING THESE CALL NUMBERS

574.52 (Parasitism in Food Chains)

591.52 (Environmental Parasitism)

593–595 (Invertebrates)

616.9 (Parasitic Diseases)

REFERENCE MATERIALS THAT MAY HELP (BOOKS OR CD-ROMS)

Buchsbaum, Ralph, et al. *Animals without Backbones*. University of Chicago Press, 1987.

Facklam, Howard and Margery Facklam. *Parasites*. Twenty-First Century Books, 1995.

Human Health. Cambridge Educational, 1997. (CD-ROM)

Invertebrates. National Geographic Society, 1998. (CD-ROM)

Olsen, O. Wilford. *Animal Parasites*. Dover Publications, 1986.

Wakelin, Derek. *Immunity to Parasites: How Parasitic Infections Are Controlled*. Cambridge University Press, 1996.

PERIODICAL INDEXES

EBSCO Magazine Article Summaries

InfoTrac

Reader's Guide to Periodical Literature

TOM Health and Science

SUGGESTED INTERNET SITES

http://www-museum.unl.edu/asp/ (American Society of Parasitologists home page)

http://www.pds.med.umich.edu/users/greenson/infectcasesmonth.html (Infectious cases of the month)

http://www.biosci.ohio-state.edu/~parasite/home.html (Parasites and parasitological resources)

http://www.pasteur.fr/Bio/parasito/Parasites.html (The Parasitology resources page)

KEY WORDS FOR PERIODICAL AND ONLINE SEARCHES

Host-Parasite Relationships

Parasites

Parasitic Diseases

Worms, Intestinal and Parasitic

Also search under other names of particular parasites and under names of particular parasitic diseases.

VIDEO PROGRAM RELATED TO THIS TOPIC

Parasites. Baker and Taylor Video, 1990.

ORGANIZATION TO CONTACT FOR ADDITIONAL INFORMATION

American Society of Parasitology. http://biology-afs.biology.uiowa.edu/

SUGGESTIONS FOR NARROWING THIS TOPIC

Create a poster illustrating the life cycle of a parasite such as the sheep liver fluke (*Fasciola hepatica*).

Discuss how parasitic infections are diagnosed.

Study the life cycle of the parasite *Schistomsoma mansoni* and report how the social habits of people contribute to its success.

RELATED TOPICS

Bacteria

Insects

Invertebrates

Viruses

This RESEARCH TOPIC GUIDE is intended to help you find information on your topic in a wide variety of sources in this and any other library. Resources, though, are not limited to those described and not all libraries will have the same titles. Please ask a librarian for further guidance.

Robotics

BACKGROUND

Robotics is the science of robots—machines which are programmed by computers to tell them what to do and which have one or more moving parts to perform specific tasks. While the idea of an inanimate object taking on human qualities and acting "alive" has been around for centuries, the first modern robots were not built until the early 1950s. Today, robots are used in industry, the medical fields, the military, the entertainment business . . . and more!

LOOK UNDER THE FOLLOWING SUBJECTS IN THE LIBRARY CATALOG

Artificial Intelligence
Industrial Robots
Robotics
Robots

BROWSE FOR BOOKS ON THE SHELF USING THESE CALL NUMBERS

006.3 (Artificial Intelligence)
621.9 (Tools and Fabricating Equipment)
629.8 (Robots)

REFERENCE MATERIALS THAT MAY HELP (BOOKS OR CD-ROMS)

Craig, John J. *Introduction to Robotics.* Addison-Wesley, 1988.
Gibilisco, Stan, ed. *The McGraw-Hill Illustrated Encyclopedia of Robotics and Artificial Intelligence.* McGraw-Hill, 1994.
Moravec, Hans. *Mind Children: The Future of Robot and Human Intelligence.* Harvard University Press, 1990.
Thro, Ellen. *Robotics: The Marriage of Computers and Machines.* Facts on File, 1993.
The Way Things Work. DK Multimedia, 1994. (CD-ROM)

PERIODICAL INDEXES

EBSCO Magazine Article Summaries
InfoTrac
Reader's Guide to Periodical Literature
TOM Health and Science

SUGGESTED INTERNET SITES

http://www.ifr.org/ (International Federation of Robotics home page)
http://www.androidworld.com/ (Android World: links to robotics, robots, animatronics, and research)

KEY WORDS FOR PERIODICAL AND ONLINE SEARCHES
 Artificial Intelligence
 Automation
 Robotics
 Robots

VIDEO PROGRAMS RELATED TO THIS TOPIC
 Artificial Intelligence. Unapix Entertainment, 1995.
 Robotic Revolution. National Geographic Educational, 1986.

ORGANIZATION TO CONTACT FOR ADDITIONAL INFORMATION
 KISS Institute for Practical Robotics, 10719 Midsummer Drive, Reston, VA
  20191. Phone: 703–620–0551, Fax: 703–860–1802. kipr@kipr.org

SUGGESTIONS FOR NARROWING THIS TOPIC
 Discuss the future of robotics, applying what robots can do today and the
  thoughts of experts and visionaries in the field of robotics.
 Research the history of robotics and robots.
 Discuss both sides of the following issue: Will robots replace people in the
  workplace?

RELATED TOPICS
 Artificial Intelligence
 Bioengineering
 Computers
 Virtual Reality

This RESEARCH TOPIC GUIDE is intended to help you find information on your topic in a wide variety of sources in this and any other library. Resources, though, are not limited to those described and not all libraries will have the same titles. Please ask a librarian for further guidance.

Science, Technology, and Society

BACKGROUND

Science and technology profoundly affect the lives of individuals and society. In our homes, schools, and places of work, the results of scientific and technological advances abound. We depend upon science and technology for our health, for our transportation, for our safety, for our entertainment, etcetera.

LOOK UNDER THE FOLLOWING SUBJECTS IN THE LIBRARY CATALOG

>   Computers and Civilization
>   Machinery in Industry
>   Science and Civilization
>   Technology and Civilization

BROWSE FOR BOOKS ON THE SHELF USING THESE CALL NUMBERS

>   303.48 (Technological Causes of Social Change)
>   306.4 (Science and Culture)
>   338 (Technology and Industry)
>   909.81 (Industrial Revolution)

REFERENCE MATERIALS THAT MAY HELP (BOOKS OR CD-ROMS)

>   Burke, James. *Connections*. Back Bay, 1995.
>   Cowan, Ruth Schwartz. *A Social History of American Technology*. Oxford University Press, 1997.
>   *DISCovering Science*. Gale Research, 1997. (CD-ROM)
>   *Eureka! Scientific Discoveries and Inventions that Shaped the World*. U.X.L., 1995.
>   Pool, Robert. *Beyond Engineering: How Society Shapes Technology*. Oxford University Press, 1997.
>   *Science and Technology Breakthroughs: 5,000 Years of Firsts*. U.X.L., 1997.
>   Stahl, Robert J. and Nancy N. Stahl. *Science and Society*. Addison-Wesley, 1995.

PERIODICAL INDEXES

>   *EBSCO Magazine Article Summaries*
>   *InfoTrac*
>   *Reader's Guide to Periodical Literature*
>   *TOM Health and Science*

SUGGESTED INTERNET SITES

>   http://www.pbs.org/wgbh/aso/ (PBS: *A Science Odyssey*)

http://www.jhuapl.edu/cybertech/ (Cyber Tech Seminars home page: Explores potential impacts on society emerging from continuing advances in information and network technology)

http://depts.washington.edu/hssexec/ (History of Science Society web page)

KEY WORDS FOR PERIODICAL AND ONLINE SEARCHES

Science and Society

Science—Social Aspects

Technology and Society

Technology—Social Aspects

VIDEO PROGRAMS RELATED TO THIS TOPIC

America On Wheels: A Social History. Turner Publishing/CNN. (Available from Time-Life Education.)

Connections (10-video series). Time-Life Video.

Connections 2. (10-video series). Time-Life Video, 1994.

ORGANIZATION TO CONTACT FOR ADDITIONAL INFORMATION

History of Science Society, Executive Office, University of Washington, Box 351330, Seattle, WA 98195–1330. Phone: 206–543–9366, Fax: 206–685–9544.

SUGGESTIONS FOR NARROWING THIS TOPIC

Discuss how a particular scientific or technological advance from a previous century impacted society.

Discuss the impact upon society of one of the following: organ transplantation, nuclear energy, computer technology, space exploration, biotechnology, genetic engineering.

Explain the influence that society has on scientific or technological advances.

RELATED TOPICS

Ethics in Science

Gender and Science

Pseudo-Science

Religion and Science

This RESEARCH TOPIC GUIDE is intended to help you find information on your topic in a wide variety of sources in this and any other library. Resources, though, are not limited to those described and not all libraries will have the same titles. Please ask a librarian for further guidance.

Solar System

BACKGROUND

Our solar system comprises the sun and the large numbers of bodies that are bound gravitationally to it and revolve around it in elliptical orbits. Some of those bodies include nine known major planets and their satellites.

LOOK UNDER THE FOLLOWING SUBJECTS IN THE LIBRARY CATALOG

Astronomy
Earth
Planets
Solar System
Sun

BROWSE FOR BOOKS ON THE SHELF USING THESE CALL NUMBERS

523.2–523.9 (Solar System)

REFERENCE MATERIALS THAT MAY HELP (BOOKS OR CD-ROMS)

Astronomy. World Book, 1997.
Astronomy & Space: From the Big Bang to the Big Crunch. U.X.L., 1997.
Becklake, Sue. *The Visual Dictionary of the Universe*. DK Publishing, 1993.
Booth, Nicholas. *Exploring the Solar System*. Cambridge University Press, 1996.
Exploring the Solar System and Beyond. National Geographic, 1995. (CD-ROM)
Solar System Explorer. Maris, 1996. (CD-ROM)

PERIODICAL INDEXES

EBSCO Magazine Article Summaries
InfoTrac
Reader's Guide to Periodical Literature
TOM Health and Science

SUGGESTED INTERNET SITES

http://www.fourmilab.ch/yoursky/ (*Your Sky*, the interactive planetarium of the web)
http://www.geocities.com/CapeCanaveral/Lab/2683 (The solar system: information on the sun and planets)
http://www.bradley.edu/las/phy/solar_system.html (The world's largest model of the solar system)

http://pds.jpl.nasa.gov/planets (Welcome to the Planets: a collection of many of the best images from NASA's planetary exploration program)

KEY WORDS FOR PERIODICAL AND ONLINE SEARCHES

Astronomy
Moon
Planets
Solar System
Sun

VIDEO PROGRAMS RELATED TO THIS TOPIC

Exploring Our Solar System. National Geographic, 1998.
Journey through the Solar System. Knowledge Unlimited, 1997.
The Solar System (4 video set). Clearvue/eav, 1994.

ORGANIZATION TO CONTACT FOR ADDITIONAL INFORMATION

NASA, Education Division, c/o Frank C. Owens, NASA Headquarters, Washington, DC 20546–0001. Phone: 202–358–1110.

SUGGESTIONS FOR NARROWING THIS TOPIC

Explain the motion of the planets around the sun.

Discuss folklore and mythology regarding the sun.

Discuss theories of how the solar system was formed.

How has the Hubble telescope helped scientists better understand our solar system?

RELATED TOPICS

Aurora (the Northern Lights)
Galaxies
Space Travel
Telescopes

This RESEARCH TOPIC GUIDE is intended to help you find information on your topic in a wide variety of sources in this and any other library. Resources, though, are not limited to those described and not all libraries will have the same titles. Please ask a librarian for further guidance.

Space Exploration

BACKGROUND

Long before the first successful manned space flight, man dreamed of traveling to the moon and planets and beyond! The first man to actually orbit the earth in a spacecraft was a Russian cosmonaut in 1961. The first American to make a space flight was Alan B. Shepard, Jr., in 1962. It was not until 1968 that a manned space flight orbited the moon, and in 1969, two Americans actually walked on the moon.

LOOK UNDER THE FOLLOWING SUBJECTS IN THE LIBRARY CATALOG

Astronauts

Outer Space—Exploration

Space Flight

Space Stations

Space Vehicles

Also search under names of particular missions, such as Space Flight to the Moon or Gemini Project.

BROWSE FOR BOOKS ON THE SHELF USING THESE CALL NUMBERS

363.12 (Spacecraft Accidents)

387.8 (Space Transportation)

500.1 (Space Sciences)

629.4–629.47 (Astronautics)

REFERENCE MATERIALS THAT MAY HELP (BOOKS OR CD-ROMS)

Baker, David. *Spaceflight and Rocketry: A Chronology.* Facts on File, 1996.

Eyewitness Encyclopedia of Space and the Universe. DK Multimedia, 1996. (CD-ROM)

Heppenheimer, T. A. *Countdown: A History of Space Flight.* John Wiley & Sons, 1997.

Launius, Roger D. *Frontiers of Space Exploration.* Greenwood, 1998.

Lee, Wayne. *To Rise from Earth: An Easy-to-Understand Guide to Space Flight.* Facts on File, 1995.

Neal, Valerie, et al. *Spaceflight: A Smithsonian Guide.* Macmillan General Reference, 1995.

Space: A Visual History of Manned Space Flight. Sumeria, 1994. (CD-ROM)

PERIODICAL INDEXES

EBSCO Magazine Article Summaries

InfoTrac

Reader's Guide to Periodical Literature

TOM Health and Science

SUGGESTED INTERNET SITES

http://liftoff.msfc.nasa.gov/ (Liftoff to space exploration)

http://www.geocities.com/CapeCanaveral/Hangar/4264/ (Terra Spacedock: Exploring space for all mankind)

http://solar.rtd.utk.edu/~mwade/alpha/alpndexe.htm (Encyclopedia Astronautica)

http://spacelink.nasa.gov/ (NASA Spacelink: An aeronautics and space resource for educators)

KEY WORDS FOR PERIODICAL AND ONLINE SEARCHES

Astronauts

Planets—Exploration

Space Exploration

Space Flight

Space Stations

Also search under specific space flights, such as Space Flight to Jupiter, Space Flight to the Moon, etcetera.

VIDEO PROGRAMS RELATED TO THIS TOPIC

Blueprint for Space: Science Fiction to Science Fact. Finley-Holiday Film, 1992.

Man on the Moon. CBS/FOX, 1989.

NASA: The First 25 Years. Goodtimes Home Video, 1987.

ORGANIZATIONS TO CONTACT FOR ADDITIONAL INFORMATION

American Astronautical Society, 6352 Rolling Mill Place, Suite #102, Springfield, VA 22152–2354. Phone: 703–866–0020, Fax 703–866–3526. info@astronautical.org

The Space Frontier Foundation, 16 First Avenue, Nyack, NY 10960. Phone: 1–800–787–7223. http://www.space-frontier.org/

SUGGESTIONS FOR NARROWING THIS TOPIC

Create a timeline which charts America's space explorations.

Discuss how robots are used in space exploration.

Discuss NASA's Hubble Space Telescope and the discoveries made possible by it.

Discuss why man should/should not explore space.

RELATED TOPICS

Astronomy

Flight

Rocketry

UFOs

This RESEARCH TOPIC GUIDE is intended to help you find information on your topic in a wide variety of sources in this and any other library. Resources, though, are not limited to those described and not all libraries will have the same titles. Please ask a librarian for further guidance.

Wildlife Conservation

BACKGROUND

Humans have wreaked havoc on the natural habitats of both plants and animals all over the world, causing many to become endangered and even extinct. Conservationists seek ways to conserve the biological diversity of our planet by protecting individual species, communities of species, and the ecosystems of which they are a part.

LOOK UNDER THE FOLLOWING SUBJECTS IN THE LIBRARY CATALOG

Conservation of Natural Resources

Endangered Species

Environmental Protection

Nature Conservation

Wildlife Conservation

Also search under names of particular plants or animals with the subheading "Protection" (example: Birds—Protection).

BROWSE FOR BOOKS ON THE SHELF USING THESE CALL NUMBERS

333.95 (Interdisciplinary Works on Biological Resources)

574.5 (Endangered Species)

639.9 (Protection of Biological Resources)

REFERENCE MATERIALS THAT MAY HELP (BOOKS OR CD-ROMS)

Bolton, M., ed. *Conservation and the Use of Wildlife Resources*. Chapman & Hall, 1997.

DeKoster, Katie. *Endangered Species: Opposing Viewpoints Digests*. Greenhaven Press, 1998.

Discovering Endangered Wildlife. LYRIQ International, 1995. (CD-ROM)

Ehrenfeld, David, ed. *Plant Conservation*. Blackwell Science, 1995.

Environment: Conservation. Mentorom Multimedia, 1995. (CD-ROM)

Patent, Dorothy Hinshaw. *Places of Refuge: Our National Wildlife Refuge System*. Clarion Books, 1992.

PERIODICAL INDEXES

EBSCO Magazine Article Summaries

InfoTrac

Reader's Guide to Periodical Literature

TOM Health and Science

SUGGESTED INTERNET SITES

http://www.nwf.org/nwf (National Wildlife Federation's home page)
http://www.audubon.org/ (National Audubon Society home page)
http://www.sierraclub.org (Sierra Club home page)

KEY WORDS FOR PERIODICAL AND ONLINE SEARCHES

Environmental Conservation & Protection
Plant Conservation
Wildlife Conservation
Wildlife Management

VIDEO PROGRAMS RELATED TO THIS TOPIC

Ancient Forests: Rage over Trees. PBS Video, 1990.
Extinction. Schlessinger Video Productions, 1993.
Where Eagles Fly. United Learning, 1994.

ORGANIZATIONS TO CONTACT FOR ADDITIONAL INFORMATION

International Wildlife Education and Conservation, 1140 Westwood Boulevard, Suite 207, Los Angeles, CA 90024. Phone: 310–0208–3631, Fax: 310–208–2779.
National Wildlife Federation, 8925 Leesburg Pike, Vienna, VA 22184. Phone: 703–790–4000.

SUGGESTIONS FOR NARROWING THIS TOPIC

Create a poster illustrating what individuals can do to help save nature's diversity.
Explain why rainforest preservation is important for our health.
Explain why species of plants and animals become endangered and how individuals can help.
Discuss laws (and penalties for breaking these laws) regarding wildlife in the United States.

RELATED TOPICS

Animal Assisted Therapy
Animal Rights
Hunting
National Parks System

This RESEARCH TOPIC GUIDE is intended to help you find information on your topic in a wide variety of sources in this and any other library. Resources, though, are not limited to those described and not all libraries will have the same titles. Please ask a librarian for further guidance.

III

Social Studies: History, Economics, and Political Science

Amendments to the Constitution/ Bill of Rights

BACKGROUND

The first ten amendments to the U.S. Constitution are called the Bill of Rights because they guarantee basic legal protection for individual rights. Congress submitted twelve amendments to the states for ratification in September of 1791, and ten of those were ratified by December 15 of that year. Since that time only seventeen more amendments to the Constitution have been ratified by the states.

LOOK UNDER THE FOLLOWING SUBJECTS IN THE LIBRARY CATALOG

Constitutional History
United States—Constitution
United States—Constitutional History
United States—History—1783–1809

BROWSE FOR BOOKS ON THE SHELF USING THESE CALL NUMBERS

342 (Constitutional History)
973.3 (United States History, 1775–1789)

REFERENCE MATERIALS THAT MAY HELP (BOOKS OR CD-ROMS)

The Constitution and Its Amendments. Macmillan Reference, 1998.
The Constitutional Amendments: 1789–1996. Gale Research, 1998.
DISCovering U.S. History. Gale Research, 1997. (CD-ROM)
Encyclopedia of the American Constitution. Macmillan, 1987. (CD-ROM)
Vile, John R. *A Companion to the United States Constitution and Its Amendments*. Praeger, 1997.
Vile, John R. *Encyclopedia of Constitutional Amendments, Proposed Amendments, and Amending Issues, 1789–1995*. ABC-CLIO, 1996.

PERIODICAL INDEXES

EBSCO Magazine Article Summaries
InfoTrac
Reader's Guide to Periodical Literature

SUGGESTED INTERNET SITES

http://www.constitution.by.net/USA/BillOfRights.html (Bill of Rights: Documents)
http://www.cs.indiana.edu/statecraft/cons.rest.html (The remaining amendments to the U.S. Constitution)

http://www.law.emory.edu/FEDERAL/usconst.html (Constitution of the United States: Links to all sections)

http://www.lsu.edu/guests/poli/public_html/const.html (The Constitution Page: Includes worldwide constitutions)

KEY WORDS FOR PERIODICAL AND ONLINE SEARCHES

Bill of Rights

United States—Constitution

VIDEO PROGRAMS RELATED TO THIS TOPIC

The Bill of Rights: A Living Document. Cambridge Educational, 1997.

Bill of Rights, Bill of Responsibilities. Bill Maher. Cambridge Educational, 1995.

The Bill of Rights in Action (3 videocassettes). American Bar Association, 1991.

SUGGESTIONS FOR NARROWING THIS TOPIC

Compare Virginia's Declaration of Rights with the U.S. Bill of Rights.

Discuss one of the following topics, using one of the amendments to the Constitution as your basis for discussion: civil rights for people with disabilities, artistic freedoms, flag burning, school prayer, gun control, militias, privacy in an electronic age.

Six amendments to the Constitution have been submitted to the states but not ratified. Relate the history behind one of them.

RELATED TOPICS

American Revolutionary War

Articles of Confederation

Declaration of Independence

U.S. Supreme Court

This RESEARCH TOPIC GUIDE is intended to help you find information on your topic in a wide variety of sources in this and any other library. Resources, though, are not limited to those described and not all libraries will have the same titles. Please ask a librarian for further guidance.

Careers

BACKGROUND

Choosing a career is one of life's most important tasks. One way young people can learn more about careers is by studying some of the many occupation-related resources available in books, video programs, and the World Wide Web.

LOOK UNDER THE FOLLOWING SUBJECTS IN THE LIBRARY CATALOG

Careers

Occupations

Vocational Guidance

Also search under names of particular careers, with the subheading "Vocational Guidance."

BROWSE FOR BOOKS ON THE SHELF USING THESE CALL NUMBERS

331.7 (Labor by Industry and Occupation)

650.14 (Success in Obtaining Jobs)

Careers in specific areas will be found in these areas, with the notation ".023" (example: careers in accounting would be found at 657.023).

REFERENCE MATERIALS THAT MAY HELP (BOOKS OR CD-ROMS)

DISCovering Careers & Jobs. Gale Research, 1997. (CD-ROM)

Encyclopedia of Careers and Vocational Guidance. J. G. Ferguson, date varies.

Encyclopedia of Careers and Vocational Guidance. Ferguson, 1997. (CD-ROM)

Occupational Outlook Handbook. Jist, date varies.

Professional Careers Sourcebook. Gale Research, 1997.

Vocational Careers Sourcebook. Gale Research, 1997.

PERIODICAL INDEXES

EBSCO Magazine Article Summaries

InfoTrac

Reader's Guide to Periodical Literature

SUGGESTED INTERNET SITES

http://careerpathsonline.com (Career Paths Online: Cyberzine on careers)

http://jobsmart.org/tools/career/spec-car.htm (JobSmart: Specific career information)

http://stats.bls.gov/ocohome.htm (Current *Occupational Outlook Handbook* online)

http://www.swep.com (School to careers resources on the Web)

KEY WORDS FOR PERIODICAL AND ONLINE SEARCHES
Careers
Occupations
Professions
Vocational Guidance

VIDEO PROGRAMS RELATED TO THIS TOPIC
Careers for the 21st Century. Delphi, 1997.
Skills for Tomorrow's Jobs (8 VHS videocassettes). Career Development, 1994.
Tech Prep Careers of the Future (5 VHS videocassettes). The School Company, 1993.

ORGANIZATION TO CONTACT FOR ADDITIONAL INFORMATION
American Vocational Association, 1410 King Street, Alexandria, VA 22314. Phone: 1–800–826–9972.

SUGGESTIONS FOR NARROWING THIS TOPIC
Explain "job shadowing." How does it help to engage young people in the world of work?

Prepare your resume, including basic biographical information, education, work experience (including volunteer work), organizations you belong to, references, and any other information which might be pertinent to a prospective employer.

Research and report on a career that interests you, focusing on the following: nature of the work, working conditions, training and education required, other qualifications, job outlook, advancement possibilities, earnings, and related occupations.

RELATED TOPICS
Job Corps
Junior Achievement
School-to-Work

This RESEARCH TOPIC GUIDE is intended to help you find information on your topic in a wide variety of sources in this and any other library. Resources, though, are not limited to those described and not all libraries will have the same titles. Please ask a librarian for further guidance.

Corporations

BACKGROUND

Researching individual corporations and the men and women who run them is a fascinating part of the study of economics and our country's history.

LOOK UNDER THE FOLLOWING SUBJECTS IN THE LIBRARY CATALOG

Business Enterprises

Corporations

BROWSE FOR BOOKS ON THE SHELF USING THESE CALL NUMBERS

338.7 (Business Enterprises and their Structure)

658.1 (Organization and Finance of Business Enterprises)

REFERENCE MATERIALS THAT MAY HELP (BOOKS OR CD-ROMS)

Multimedia Business 500. Allegro, 1995. (CD-ROM)

Fortune Guide to the 500 Largest U.S. Corporations. Warner Books, 1996.

Hoover's 500: Profiles of America's Largest Business Enterprises. Hoover's, 1996.

Hoover's Emerging Companies 1995: Profiles of America's Most Exciting Growth Enterprises. Time Warner Electronic, 1995. (CD-ROM)

International Directory of Company Histories (multi-volumes). St. James Press, 1988–present (continuously updated).

United States Corporation Histories. Garland, 1991.

PERIODICAL INDEXES

EBSCO Magazine Article Summaries

InfoTrac

Reader's Guide to Periodical Literature

SUGGESTED INTERNET SITES

http://www.businesswire.com/ (Business Wire 1998: Search current headlines for business information)

http://www.refdesk.com/stocks.html (My Virtual Reference Desk: Stock Market)

http://pathfinder.com/fortune/ (*Fortune* online: Current business articles)

KEY WORDS FOR PERIODICAL AND ONLINE SEARCHES

Business Enterprises

Companies

Corporate History

Corporations

VIDEO PROGRAMS RELATED TO THIS TOPIC

Andrew Carnegie: The Original Man of Steel. (Available from Zenger Media.)

Monopoly/Oligopolies. Annenberg/CPB Collection, 1992.

Work in Progress. CNN, 1993.

ORGANIZATIONS TO CONTACT FOR ADDITIONAL INFORMATION

Council of Better Business Bureaus. http://www.bb.org/

United States Chamber of Commerce, 1615 H Street, N.W., Washington, DC 20062. Phone: 202–659–6000, Fax: 202–463–3190.

SUGGESTIONS FOR NARROWING THIS TOPIC

Research the history of one of the top fifty businesses in America.

Write a biographical sketch of one of the nation's leading CEOs.

Discuss the qualities that make a company successful.

RELATED TOPICS

Careers

Corporate Crime

Stock Market

Women in the Workplace

This RESEARCH TOPIC GUIDE is intended to help you find information on your topic in a wide variety of sources in this and any other library. Resources, though, are not limited to those described and not all libraries will have the same titles. Please ask a librarian for further guidance.

French Revolution

BACKGROUND

On July 14, 1789, a Parisian mob attacked the Bastille, marking the beginning of the French Revolution, a peasant's revolt against the French aristocracy that led to the Reign of Terror and the execution of the King and Queen of France, plus countless other members of the aristocracy and enemies of the Revolution, including women and children.

LOOK UNDER THE FOLLOWING SUBJECT IN THE LIBRARY CATALOG

France—History—1789–1799, Revolution

BROWSE FOR BOOKS ON THE SHELF USING THIS CALL NUMBER

944.04 (Revolutionary Period of French History)

REFERENCE MATERIALS THAT MAY HELP (BOOKS OR CD-ROMS)

Carlyle, Thomas, et al. *The French Revolution: A History*. Oxford University Press, 1989.

DISCovering World History. Gale Research, 1997. (CD-ROM)

Doyle, William. *The Oxford History of the French Revolution*. Oxford University Press, 1990.

The French Revolution. Clearvue/eav. (CD-ROM)

Oftinoski, Steven. *Triumph and Terror: The French Revolution*. Facts on File, 1993.

Schama, Simon and Luann Walther. *Citizens: A Chronicle of the French Revolution*. Random House, 1990.

Stewart, Gail B. *Life during the French Revolution*. Lucent Books, 1995.

PERIODICAL INDEXES

EBSCO Magazine Article Summaries

Index to *History Today* Magazine

InfoTrac

Reader's Guide to Periodical Literature

SUGGESTED INTERNET SITES

http://history.hanover.edu/modern/frenchrv.htm (The French Revolution: Links to primary and secondary sources on the internet: Hanover College History Department) http://www.geocities.com/Athens/Forum/9790/index.html (Blake's Bastille: features William Blake's "The French Revolution." Includes a cyber tour of La Bastille)

http://www.britannia.com/history/euro/1/2_2.html (The ideology of the French Revolution)

KEY WORDS FOR PERIODICAL AND ONLINE SEARCHES

France—History—Revolution, 1789–1799

French Revolution

VIDEO PROGRAMS RELATED TO THIS TOPIC

The French Revolution. Clearvue, 1989.

The French Revolution. Coronet, 1975.

The French Revolution and Napoleon. New York Times.

ORGANIZATION TO CONTACT FOR ADDITIONAL INFORMATION

Napoleonic Association, c/o Helen Bell, 13 Dorset Place, Faversham, Kent ME13 8PP. Phone: 017–955–30763. http://www.n-a.co.uk/nacont.htm

SUGGESTIONS FOR NARROWING THIS TOPIC

Compare and contrast the American and French Revolutions.

Create an annotated timeline illustrating important events leading up to and including the French Revolution.

Discuss the aftermath and consequences of the French Revolution.

Discuss the causes of the French Revolution.

RELATED TOPICS

The American Revolution

French and Indian Wars

Kings and Queens of France

This RESEARCH TOPIC GUIDE is intended to help you find information on your topic in a wide variety of sources in this and any other library. Resources, though, are not limited to those described and not all libraries will have the same titles. Please ask a librarian for further guidance.

Great Depression

BACKGROUND
Following a decade of prosperity and wild stock market speculation, Black Thursday, October 29, 1929, when the Stock Market crashed, marked the beginning of the worst economic slump in U.S. history—the Great Depression.

LOOK UNDER THE FOLLOWING SUBJECTS IN THE LIBRARY CATALOG
Economic Depressions
United States—History—1919–1933
United States—History—1933–1945

BROWSE FOR BOOKS ON THE SHELF USING THESE CALL NUMBERS
338.5 (Economic depressions)
973.91–973.917 (U.S. History during the Great Depression)

REFERENCE MATERIALS THAT MAY HELP (BOOKS OR CD-ROMS)
Burg, David F. *The Great Depression: An Eyewitness History*. Facts on File, 1996.
Farrell, Jacqueline. *The Great Depression*. Lucent Books, 1996.
Fremon, David K. *The Great Depression in American History*. Enslow, 1997.
The Great Depression. Clearvue/eav, n.d. (CD-ROM)
Meltzer, Milton. *Brother, Can You Spare a Dime? The Great Depression 1929–1933*. Facts on File, 1991.
Nishi, Dennis. *Life during the Great Depression*. Lucent Books, 1998.
Ross, Stewart. *Causes and Consequences of the Great Depression*. Raintree/Steck-Vaughn, 1998.

PERIODICAL INDEXES
EBSCO Magazine Article Summaries
Index to *History Today* Magazine
InfoTrac
Reader's Guide to Periodical Literature

SUGGESTED INTERNET SITES
http://rs6.loc.gov/wpaintro/wpahome.html (WPA Life Histories home page)
http://newdeal.feri.org/ (New Deal Network)
http://www.mcsc.k12.in.us/mhs/social/madedo (We Made Do: Recalling the Great Depression)

http://www.studyweb.com/culture/amer/thirties.htm (The Great Depression: numerous links)

KEY WORDS FOR PERIODICAL AND ONLINE SEARCHES

Business Depression, 1929–1939
Economic Depression, 1929–1939
Great Depression, 1929–1939
United States—History—Depression and New Deal (1929–1939)

VIDEO PROGRAMS RELATED TO THIS TOPIC

The Great Depression. Guidance Associates, 1989.
The Great Depression. A & E Home Video, 1998.
The Great Depression and the New Deal. Schlessinger, 1996.

SUGGESTIONS FOR NARROWING THIS TOPIC

Create an annotated timeline illustrating events leading up to and including the Great Depression, beginning with 1920 and ending with the start of World War II in 1939.

Describe how the Great Depression affected the everyday life of the average American.

Discuss programs set up by the government to give work to the millions of people unemployed in the 1930s, including Social Security, the Works Progress Administration (WPA), the Rural Electrification Administration (REA), and the Wagner Act of 1935.

RELATED TOPICS

Dust Bowl
Poverty
Roaring Twenties
Stock Market

This RESEARCH TOPIC GUIDE is intended to help you find information on your topic in a wide variety of sources in this and any other library. Resources, though, are not limited to those described and not all libraries will have the same titles. Please ask a librarian for further guidance.

Greece, Ancient

BACKGROUND

Over 2000 years ago Ancient Greece flourished as a civilization that is lauded even today as founders of Western civilization. Their government, their advances in science, their skill in the arts, their accomplishments in athletics, and their great men of the arts and philosophy all left their mark throughout the ages.

LOOK UNDER THE FOLLOWING SUBJECTS IN THE LIBRARY CATALOG

> Greece—Antiquities
> Greece—History—0–323
> Greek Civilization

BROWSE FOR BOOKS ON THE SHELF USING THESE CALL NUMBERS

> 709.38 (Greek Art)
> 733 (Greek Sculpture)
> 913.8 (Ancient Greece—Description and Travel)
> 938 (History of Ancient Greece)

REFERENCE MATERIALS THAT MAY HELP (BOOKS OR CD-ROMS)

> *Athena: Classical Mythology*. Macmillan, 1995. (CD-ROM)
> Durando, Furio. *Ancient Greece: The Dawn of the Western World*. Stewart Tabori and Chang, 1997.
> Garland, Robert. *Daily Life of the Ancient Greeks*. Greenwood, 1998.
> Grant, Michael and Rachel Kitzinger. *Civilization of the Ancient Mediterranean: Greece and Rome*. Charles Scribner's Sons, 1989.
> Martin, Thomas R. *Ancient Greece: From Prehistoric to Hellenistic Times*. Yale University Press, 1996.
> Sacks, David. *Encyclopedia of the Ancient Greek World*. Facts on File, 1995.

PERIODICAL INDEXES

> *EBSCO Magazine Article Summaries*
> Index to *History Today* Magazine
> Index to *National Geographic Magazine*
> *InfoTrac*
> *Reader's Guide to Periodical Literature*

SUGGESTED INTERNET SITES

> http://www.pbs.org/mpt/alexander (Home Page *Alexander the Great*, with Michael Wood, from PBS)
> http://www.uky.edu/ArtsSciences/Classics/gender.html (Women and gender in the ancient world)

http://hydra.perseus.tufts.edu/ (Home page of the Perseus Project)

KEY WORDS FOR PERIODICAL AND ONLINE SEARCHES
Ancient Greece—History
Greece—Civilization
Greece—History

VIDEO PROGRAMS RELATED TO THIS TOPIC
Ancient Greece (2 video programs). Kultur Video, 1995.
Athens and Ancient Greece. Questar Video Communications, 1995.
Greeks (2 videocassettes). Films Incorporated, 1993.

SUGGESTIONS FOR NARROWING THIS TOPIC
Create an annotated timeline reviewing the life and deeds of Alexander the Great.
Discuss accomplishments of the Ancient Greeks in one of the following areas: The Arts, Education, Government, Science, or Sports.
Explain the Ptolemaic world view.
Research daily life in Ancient Greece.

RELATED TOPICS
Ancient Rome
Gods and Goddesses
Pompeii
Trojan War

This RESEARCH TOPIC GUIDE is intended to help you find information on your topic in a wide variety of sources in this and any other library. Resources, though, are not limited to those described and not all libraries will have the same titles. Please ask a librarian for further guidance.

Indian Removal

BACKGROUND

When Europeans first came to North America, there were approximately one million Indians living in what was to become the United States. By 1890, fewer than 350,000 had survived the white man's effort to erradicate them. The Indian Removal Act of 1830, the Indian Wars, and the Dawes Act of 1887 had defeated the proud first Americans, stripping them of their tribal lands and destroying their way of life.

LOOK UNDER THE FOLLOWING SUBJECTS IN THE LIBRARY CATALOG

 Indians of North America

 Indians of North America—Government Relations

 Indians of North America—Reservations

BROWSE FOR BOOKS ON THE SHELF USING THESE CALL NUMBERS

 323.1 (Civil Rights of Native Americans)

 970.004 (North American Native Peoples)

 970.1 (North American Native Peoples, optional call number)

REFERENCE MATERIALS THAT MAY HELP (BOOKS OR CD-ROMS)

 The American Indians: A Multimedia Encyclopedia. Facts on File, 1996. (CD-ROM)

 Anderson, William L., ed. *Cherokee Removal Before and After*. University of Georgia Press, 1991.

 Hoig, Stanley. *Night of the Cruel Moon: Cherokee Removal and the Trail of Tears*. Facts on File, 1996.

 Keenan, Jerry. *Encyclopedia of American Indian Wars, 1492–1890*. ABC-CLIO, 1997.

 Olson, James S. *Encyclopedia of American Indian Civil Rights*. Greenwood, 1997.

 Through Indian Eyes: The Untold Story of Native American Peoples. Reader's Digest, 1995.

PERIODICAL INDEXES

 EBSCO Magazine Article Summaries

 Index to *American Heritage* Magazine

 InfoTrac

 Reader's Guide to Periodical Literature

SUGGESTED INTERNET SITES

 http://members.xoom.com/eaglewing/cheyenne.htm (Introduction to the Cheyenne Nation) http://pages.tca.net/martikw/ (History of the Cherokee)

http://lawlibrary.uoregon.edu/sub-indigenous.html (Native American Indians and other indigenous peoples)

KEY WORDS FOR PERIODICAL AND ONLINE SEARCHES

Indians of North America

Indians of North America—Government Relations

Also search under names of particular Native American tribes.

VIDEO PROGRAMS RELATED TO THIS TOPIC

Fight No More Forever. PBS, 1996.

Native Americans: The History of a People. Knowledge Unlimited, 1992.

One Sky above Us. PBS, 1996.

ORGANIZATIONS TO CONTACT FOR ADDITIONAL INFORMATION

Cherokee National Historical Society, Inc., PO Box 515, Tahlequah, OK 74465–0515. Phone: 918–456–6007, Fax: 918–456–6165.

Department of the Interior, Bureau of Indian Affairs, Office of Public Affairs, 1849 C Street, N.W., Washington, DC 20240–0001. Phone: 202–208–3711, Fax: 202–501–1516. http://www.doi.gov/bureau-indian-affairs.html

SUGGESTIONS FOR NARROWING THIS TOPIC

Research the Indian Removal from Indiana to Kansas in 1846, a process that began with the Battle of Mississinewa in December of 1812.

Research U.S. government–Native American treaties made and broken between 1850 and 1900.

Research the hardships suffered during the Indian Removal known as the "Trail of Tears."

RELATED TOPICS

Contributions of Native Americans

Mounds and Mound Builders

Navajo "Codetalkers" of World War II

This RESEARCH TOPIC GUIDE is intended to help you find information on your topic in a wide variety of sources in this and any other library. Resources, though, are not limited to those described and not all libraries will have the same titles. Please ask a librarian for further guidance.

Industrial Revolution

BACKGROUND

The Industrial Revolution, which began in England in the early 1700s with inventions such as the cotton mill, which made mass production possible, was characterized by dramatic social and economic change.

LOOK UNDER THE FOLLOWING SUBJECTS IN THE LIBRARY CATALOG

> Great Britain—History—1800–1899
> Industrial Revolution
> Industrialization
> Industry—History

BROWSE FOR BOOKS ON THE SHELF USING THESE CALL NUMBERS

> 330.9 (Economic Situation and Conditions)
> 909.81 (Industrial Revolution)

REFERENCE MATERIALS THAT MAY HELP (BOOKS OR CD-ROMS)

> Ashton, Thomas S. *The Industrial Revolution, 1760–1830*. Oxford University Press, 1998.
> Clare, John D., ed. *Industrial Revolution*. Gulliver Books, 1994.
> Corrick, James A. *The Industrial Revolution*. Lucent Books, 1998.
> *The Industrial Revolution*. Clearvue/eav. (CD-ROM)
> Lines, Clifford John and Barrie Trinder. *Companion to the Industrial Revolution*. Facts on File, 1990.
> Stearns, Peter N. and John H. Hinshaw. *ABC-CLIO World History Companion to the Industrial Revolution*. ABC-CLIO, 1996.

PERIODICAL INDEXES

> *EBSCO Magazine Article Summaries*
> Index to *American Heritage* Magazine
> Index to *History Today* Magazine
> *InfoTrac*
> *Reader's Guide to Periodical Literature*

SUGGESTED INTERNET SITES

> http://www.stg.brown.edu/projects/hypertext/landow/victorian/history/hist8.html (Child labor during the Industrial Revolution)
> http://ab.edu/~delcol_l/worker.html (Life of 19th century workers)

http://www.darex.com/indurevo.htm (A short history of machine tools: the two countries that invented the Industrial Revolution)

http://www.history.rochester.edu/steam (The steam engine library: searchable)

KEY WORDS FOR PERIODICAL AND ONLINE SEARCHES

Great Britain—Economic Conditions—1760–1860

Great Britain—History—18th Century

Industrial Revolution

VIDEO PROGRAMS RELATED TO THIS TOPIC

The Industrial Revolution. Educational Video Network, 1995.

The Industrial Revolution. United Learning, 1994.

The Industrial Revolution in America. Guidance Associates.

SUGGESTIONS FOR NARROWING THIS TOPIC

Discuss how the Industrial Revolution changed agriculture and rural life.

Discuss the role children played during the Industrial Revolution.

Discuss some of the inventions that made the Industrial Revolution possible.

Discuss working conditions in factories during the Industrial Revolution.

Discuss the Industrial Revolution's effects on society.

RELATED TOPICS

Capitalism

Labor Unions

Technology

This RESEARCH TOPIC GUIDE is intended to help you find information on your topic in a wide variety of sources in this and any other library. Resources, though, are not limited to those described and not all libraries will have the same titles. Please ask a librarian for further guidance.

Labor Movement in America

BACKGROUND

A labor movement is defined as "the efforts of workers as a group to improve their economic position" (*World Book Encyclopedia*). The labor movement in America has its roots in the early trade unions of the 1600s.

LOOK UNDER THE FOLLOWING SUBJECTS IN THE LIBRARY CATALOG

Collective Bargaining

Labor Disputes

Labor Movement

Labor Unions

Strikes

BROWSE FOR BOOKS ON THE SHELF USING THESE CALL NUMBERS

322 (Labor Movement)

331.8 (Labor Unions)

658.3 (Collective Bargaining)

REFERENCE MATERIALS THAT MAY HELP (BOOKS OR CD-ROMS)

DISCovering U.S. History. Gale Research, 1997. (CD-ROM)

Ferriss, Susan, et al. *The Fight in the Fields: Cesar Chavez and the Farmworkers Movement*. Harcourt Brace, 1997.

Fisher, Leonard Everett. *The Unions*. Holiday House, 1982.

Flagler, John J. *The Labor Movement in the United States*. Lerner, 1990.

Galenson, Walter. *The American Labor Movement, 1955–1995*. Greenwood, 1996.

Taylor, Paul F. *The ABC-CLIO Companion to the American Labor Movement*. ABC-CLIO, 1993.

PERIODICAL INDEXES

EBSCO Magazine Article Summaries

Index to *American Heritage* Magazine

InfoTrac

Reader's Guide to Periodical Literature

SUGGESTED INTERNET SITES

http://www.aflcio.org/home.htm (Home page of AFL-CIO labor union)

http://www.inform.umd.edu/HIST/Gompers/web1.html (A documentary history of the American working class)

http://www.unionweb.org/history.htm (A short history of American labor)

http://www.igc.org/igc/labornet (Labornet: Labor news and information)

KEY WORDS FOR PERIODICAL AND ONLINE SEARCHES

Labor Movement

Labor Unions

Strikes

Trade Unions

Also search under names of particular labor unions.

VIDEO PROGRAMS RELATED TO THIS TOPIC

The Masses and the Millionaires. Learning Corporation of America, 1973.

Norma Rae. 20th Century Fox, 1979.

Organizing America. Cambridge, 1994.

ORGANIZATIONS TO CONTACT FOR ADDITIONAL INFORMATION

International Labor Organization, Washington Branch Office, 1828 L Street, NW, Suite 801, Washington, DC 20036.

National Labor Committee, 275 7th Avenue, 15th Floor, New York, NY 10001. Phone: 212–242–3002.

SUGGESTIONS FOR NARROWING THIS TOPIC

Create an annotated timeline illustrating significant events in the American Labor Movement.

Discuss Cesar Estrada Chavez's struggles to fight for the rights of farm workers around the world.

Discuss significant legislative accomplishments for labor.

Relate some examples of modern-times resistance to unions by government and employers.

Research the history of Labor Day.

RELATED TOPICS

Child Labor

Indentured Servitude

Industrial Revolution

Migrant Workers

This RESEARCH TOPIC GUIDE is intended to help you find information on your topic in a wide variety of sources in this and any other library. Resources, though, are not limited to those described and not all libraries will have the same titles. Please ask a librarian for further guidance.

Lewis and Clark Expedition

BACKGROUND

Meriwether Lewis and William Clark were commissioned by President Thomas Jefferson in 1803 to explore the Missouri River with the purpose of finding a water route to the Pacific Ocean and establishing an American presence west of the sixteen states of the United States.

LOOK UNDER THE FOLLOWING SUBJECTS IN THE LIBRARY CATALOG

> Lewis and Clark Expedition
> United States—Exploring Expeditions
> United States—History—1783–1809

BROWSE FOR BOOKS ON THE SHELF USING THIS CALL NUMBER

> 973.4 (U.S. History, 1789–1809)

REFERENCE MATERIALS THAT MAY HELP (BOOKS OR CD-ROMS)

> *American Journal Series*. MicroMedia, 1996. (CD-ROM)
> Blumberg, Rhoda. *The Incredible Journey of Lewis and Clark*. Beech Tree Books, 1995.
> *DISCovering U.S. History*. Gale Research, 1997. (CD-ROM)
> Lewis, Meriwether and William Clark. *The Journals of Lewis and Clark*. New American Library, 1964.
> Twist, Clint. *Lewis and Clark: Exploring North America*. Raintree Steck-Vaughn, 1994.

PERIODICAL INDEXES

> *EBSCO Magazine Article Summaries*
> Index to *American Heritage* Magazine
> *InfoTrac*
> *Reader's Guide to Periodical Literature*

SUGGESTED INTERNET SITES

> http://www.lewis-clark.org (Discovering Lewis and Clark: home page)
> http://www.olypen.com/gillde/lance/bibliographies/lewis.htm (Lewis and Clark Expedition annotated bibliography)
> http://www.lewisandclark.org/index.htm (Home page of the Lewis and Clark Trail Heritage Foundation)
> http://www.pbs.org/lewisandclark/ (From PBS Online: Lewis and Clark—journals, timeline, map, interactive story, etcetera)

KEY WORDS FOR PERIODICAL AND ONLINE SEARCHES

Lewis and Clark Expedition

West (U.S.)

U.S.—Discovery and Exploration

VIDEO PROGRAMS RELATED TO THIS TOPIC

Expansionism. Schlessinger, 1996.

The Lewis and Clark Expedition. United Learning, 1992.

We Proceeded On . . . The Expedition of Lewis and Clark. Kaw Valley Films, 1991.

ORGANIZATION TO CONTACT FOR ADDITIONAL INFORMATION

Lewis and Clark Trail Heritage Foundation, Inc., PO Box 3434, Great Falls, MT 59403.

SUGGESTIONS FOR NARROWING THIS TOPIC

Discuss the expedition's encounters with Native Americans.

Discuss medical precautions undertaken by the expedition.

Discuss Sacagawea's contributions to the expedition.

RELATED TOPICS

The California Gold Rush

The Donner Party

Frontier Life in the Early to Mid-1800s

Manifest Destiny

This RESEARCH TOPIC GUIDE is intended to help you find information on your topic in a wide variety of sources in this and any other library. Resources, though, are not limited to those described and not all libraries will have the same titles. Please ask a librarian for further guidance.

The Middle Ages

BACKGROUND

The Middle Ages, also known as the Medieval period of history, covered the period of Western civilization from the fall of the Roman Empire to the Italian Renaissance—nearly 1,000 years between A.D. 950 to A.D. 1500.

LOOK UNDER THE FOLLOWING SUBJECTS IN THE LIBRARY CATALOG

Europe—History—476–1492
Feudalism
Medieval Civilization
Middle Ages

BROWSE FOR BOOKS ON THE SHELF USING THESE CALL NUMBERS

394 (General Customs)
909 (World History)
940.1 (History of Europe to 1453)

REFERENCE MATERIALS THAT MAY HELP (BOOKS OR CD-ROMS)

A general encyclopedia such as *World Book Encyclopedia, Encyclopedia Americana, Collier's Encyclopedia*, or *Encyclopedia Britannica.*
Bunson, Matthew E. *Encyclopedia of the Middle Ages.* Facts on File, 1995.
DISCovering World History. Gale, 1997. (CD-ROM)
The Early Middle Ages. Raintree/Steck-Vaughn, 1990.
Fossier, Robert. *The Cambridge Illustrated History of the Middle Ages.* Cambridge University Press, 1998.
Kenyon, Sherrilyn. *The Writer's Guide to Everyday Life in the Middle Ages.* Writer's Digest Books, 1995.
The Late Middle Ages. Raintree/Steck-Vaughn, 1990.

PERIODICAL INDEXES

EBSCO Magazine Article Summaries
Index to *History Today* Magazine
InfoTrac
Reader's Guide to Periodical Literature

SUGGESTED INTERNET SITES

http://history.evansville.net/medieval.html (The Development of Western Civilization: Medieval World)
http://netserf.cua.edu (NetSerf: The Internet connection for Medieval resources)

http://www.btinternet.com/~timeref/ (A database of Medieval events, people, and places)

http://members.aol.com/tmatrust/home.html (The Middle Ages Trust: A site for the digital community to study the Medieval period)

KEY WORDS FOR PERIODICAL AND ONLINE SEARCHES

Civilization, Medieval

Knights and Knighthood

Medieval World History

Middle Ages

VIDEO PROGRAMS RELATED TO THIS TOPIC

Castles: The Glory of the Middle Ages. Double Diamond, 1993.

Medieval Times: 1000–1450. United Learning, 1992.

Western World History: Medieval Times (5 videocassettes: *Chaucer and the Medieval Period, The Nobility, The Villagers, Guilds and Trades*, and *The Role of the Church*). Coronet.

ORGANIZATIONS TO CONTACT FOR ADDITIONAL INFORMATION

Arizona Center for Medieval and Renaissance Studies, Arizona State University, PO Box 872301, Tempe, AZ 85287–2301.

The Realm of Chivalry, PO Box 23334, Federal Way, WA 98093–0334.

The Texas Medieval Association, c/o Don Kagay, Department of History, Albany State College, Albany, GA 31705.

SUGGESTIONS FOR NARROWING THIS TOPIC

Discuss the Germanic Invasions, which marked the beginnings of the Middle Ages.

Discuss the causes, course, and effects on society of the plague, also called the "Black Death."

Discuss and describe weapons, armor, and warfare during the Middle Ages.

Research one aspect of the Middle Ages, such as the Church's influence, life in a castle, medieval towns, or everyday life.

RELATED TOPICS

Chivalry

The Knights Templar

The Magna Carta

The Mongol Invasion of Europe

The Vikings

This RESEARCH TOPIC GUIDE is intended to help you find information on your topic in a wide variety of sources in this and any other library. Resources, though, are not limited to those described and not all libraries will have the same titles. Please ask a librarian for further guidance.

Migrant Workers in America

BACKGROUND

Industrialization created good paying jobs in cities, luring many laborers away from lower paying farm jobs. Migrant workers, who move around in a seasonal pattern looking for work, met the need for cheap labor on farms to harvest the crops.

LOOK UNDER THE FOLLOWING SUBJECTS IN THE LIBRARY CATALOG

Agricultural Laborers

Migrant Labor

BROWSE FOR BOOKS ON THE SHELF USING THESE CALL NUMBERS

331.5 (Migrant Workers)

362.85 (Problems of and Services to Migrant Workers)

REFERENCE MATERIALS THAT MAY HELP (BOOKS OR CD-ROMS)

Altman, Linda J. *Migrant Farm Workers: The Temporary People*. Franklin Watts, 1994.

DeRuiz, Dana C. and Richard Larios. *LA Causa: The Migrant Farmworkers' Story*. Raintree/Steck-Vaughn, 1992.

Encyclopedia of Social Issues. Marshall Cavendish, 1997.

Ferriss, Susan, et al. *The Fight in the Fields: Cesar Chavez and the Farmworkers Movement*. Harcourt Brace, 1997.

Rothenberg, David and Robert Coles. *With These Hands: An Oral Portrait of Migrant Farmworkers*. Harcourt Brace, 1998.

Voices of the 30s. Sunburst, 1994. (CD-ROM)

PERIODICAL INDEXES

EBSCO Magazine Article Summaries

Index to *American Heritage* Magazine

InfoTrac

Reader's Guide to Periodical Literature

SUGGESTED INTERNET SITES

http://www.mhsqic.org (Migrant Head Start Quality Improvement Center home page)

http://naid.sppsr.ucla.edu/mix.html (Mixtec Migrant Farm—articles on healthcare services, migrant families, farm labor advocates, etcetera)

http://www.ncfh.org/index.html (Home Page of Office of Migrant Education, U.S. Department of Education)

KEY WORDS FOR PERIODICAL AND ONLINE SEARCHES
Migrant Agricultural Laborers
Migrant Labor
Migrant Workers

VIDEO PROGRAMS RELATED TO THIS TOPIC
The Grapes of Wrath. 20th Century Fox, 1940.
Harvest of Shame. CBS, 1960.
The Migrants. CBS, 1973.

ORGANIZATIONS TO CONTACT FOR ADDITIONAL INFORMATION
National Center for Farmworker Health, Inc., 1515 Capital of Texas Highway South, Suite 220, Austin, TX 78746. Phone: 512–328–7682, Fax: 512–328–8559.

Office of Migrant Education, U.S. Department of Education. http://www.ed.gov/OESE/MEP/index.html

SUGGESTIONS FOR NARROWING THIS TOPIC
Discuss health problems of migrant workers.
Discuss living and working conditions among migrant workers in California.
Discuss federal laws concerning migrant labor.
Make a graph illlustrating the ethnic distribution of America's migrant workers.

RELATED TOPICS
Dust Bowl
Great Depression
Immigration
Labor Unions

This RESEARCH TOPIC GUIDE is intended to help you find information on your topic in a wide variety of sources in this and any other library. Resources, though, are not limited to those described and not all libraries will have the same titles. Please ask a librarian for further guidance.

National Parks

BACKGROUND

The Yellowstone National Park Act of 1872 set aside public lands for public enjoyment and opened the way for the creation of the National Park Service. Today, the National Park System encompasses approximately 80.7 million acres for the benefit and enjoyment of the people.

LOOK UNDER THE FOLLOWING SUBJECTS IN THE LIBRARY CATALOG

National Monuments
National Parks and Reserves
Public Lands
Wilderness Areas

Also search under names of individual national parks.

BROWSE FOR BOOKS USING THESE CALL NUMBERS

363.6 (Public Park and Recreation Services)
719 (Natural Monuments; Forest and Wildlife Reserves)
917.3 (Geography of and Travel in the United States)

REFERENCE MATERIALS THAT MAY HELP (BOOKS OR CD-ROMS)

Exploring America's National Parks. Rand McNally, 1998.
Kraulis, J. A., et al. *From Acadia to Yellowstone: The National Parks of the United States*. Smithmark, 1996.
Little, Charles E., et al. *Discover America; The Smithsonian Book of the National Parks*. Smithsonian Institute, 1996.
National Parks 3.0. Cambrix, 1997. (CD-ROM)
Newhouse, Elizabeth, ed. *National Geographic's Guide to the National Parks of the United States*. National Geographic Society, 1997.
World Book's Information Finder. World Book, date varies. (CD-ROM Encyclopedia)

PERIODICAL INDEXES TO SEARCH (BOOKS OR CD-ROMS)

EBSCO Magazine Article Summaries
Index to *National Geographic Magazine*
InfoTrac
Reader's Guide to Periodical Literature

SUGGESTED INTERNET SITES

http://www.nationalparks.org/guide/us_map.htm (National Park Foundation: Guide to America's national parks. Locate parks by name, state, or region.)
http://www.nps.gov/ (ParkNet: The National Park Service "Place on the Web")

http://www.coolworks.com/natprk.htm (Jobs in national parks, preserves, monuments, recreation, and wilderness areas.)

http://www.npca.org/home/npca (Home page of the National Parks and Conservation Association)

KEY WORDS FOR PERIODICAL AND ONLINE SEARCHES

Names of Individual Parks

National Park Service

National Parks

Parks and Campgrounds

VIDEO PROGRAMS RELATED TO THIS TOPIC

America's Great National Parks. University of Georgia, 1995.

America's National Parks. International Video Network, 1994.

Celebrated National Parks. International Video Network, 1995.

ORGANIZATIONS TO CONTACT FOR ADDITIONAL INFORMATION

National Park Foundation, 1101 17th Street, NW, Suite 1102, Washington, DC 20036–4704. Phone: 202–785–4500.

National Park Service, 1849 C Street, NW, Washington, DC 20240. Phone: 202–208–6843.

SUGGESTIONS FOR NARROWING THIS TOPIC

Create a brochure for one our nation's national parks, giving a brief history, points of interest, admission cost, hours, and other pertinent tourist information.

Indicate our nation's national parks on a U.S. map.

Explain the criteria for an area to become designated as a national park.

Research the history of the National Park System.

SUGGESTIONS FOR RELATED TOPICS

Conservation

Ecology

State Parks

Zoos

This RESEARCH TOPIC GUIDE is intended to help you find information on your topic in a wide variety of sources in this and any other library. Resources, though, are not limited to those described and not all libraries will have the same titles. Please ask a librarian for further guidance.

NATO (North Atlantic Treaty Organization)

BACKGROUND

The North Atlantic Treaty Organization (NATO) was established in 1950 for the common defense of its then 12 member nations, providing for a collective defense against a possible attack by another nation. There are now 16 nations which belong to the alliance, and there is a continuing debate concerning adding more members.

LOOK UNDER THE FOLLOWING SUBJECTS IN THE LIBRARY CATALOG

International Relations
International Security
North Atlantic Treaty Organization
United States—Foreign Relations

BROWSE FOR BOOKS ON THE SHELF USING THESE CALL NUMBERS

341.2 (International Organizations)
341.3 (International Relations)
341.7 (Law of International Cooperation)

REFERENCE MATERIALS THAT MAY HELP (BOOKS OR CD-ROMS)

Chronicle of the 20th Century. Dorling Kindersley, 1996.
Heller, Francis H. and John R. Gillingham, eds. *NATO: The Founding of the Atlantic Alliance and the Integration of Europe*. St. Martin's Press, 1992.
Kaplan, Lawrence S. *NATO and the United States: The Enduring Alliance*. Twayne, 1994.
Solomon, Gerald B. *The NATO Enlargement Debate, 1990–1997: Blessings of Liberty*. Praeger, 1998.
Ziring, Lawrence, et al. *International Relations: A Political Dictionary*. ABC-CLIO, 1995.

PERIODICAL INDEXES

EBSCO Magazine Article Summaries
InfoTrac
Reader's Guide to Periodical Literature

SUGGESTED INTERNET SITES

http://www.saclant.nato.int/ (NATO-SACLANT—Supreme Allied Commander, Atlantic: Biographies, fact sheets, upcoming events, recent events, NATO links, career openings, national days, etc.)

http://www.nato.int/ (Official home page of NATO—Includes a virtual visit to North Atlantic Council)

KEY WORDS FOR PERIODICAL AND ONLINE SERCHES
International Security
NATO
North Atlantic Treaty Organization

VIDEO PROGRAMS RELATED TO THIS TOPIC
Talking Peace with Jimmy Carter. Close Up Foundation, 1995.
The Ugly American. Universal, 1963.

ORGANIZATION TO CONTACT FOR ADDITIONAL INFORMATION
Allied Command Atlantic, Attn.: Public Information Office, 7857 Blandy Road, Suite 100, Norfolk, VA 23551–2490. Phone: 757–445–2490, Fax: 757–445–3234.

SUGGESTIONS FOR NARROWING THIS TOPIC
Create a chart showing all sixteen of NATO's members, heads of their governments, and representatives to NATO.
Discuss the structure of NATO.
Discuss pros and cons of NATO enlargement.
Research the history and purpose of NATO.

RELATED TOPICS
Global Development
International Trade
United Nations
World Refugees

This RESEARCH TOPIC GUIDE is intended to help you find information on your topic in a wide variety of sources in this and any other library. Resources, though, are not limited to those described and not all libraries will have the same titles. Please ask a librarian for further guidance.

Prehistoric Man

BACKGROUND

The earliest human-like remains have been found in Africa, the most famous being "Lucy," a three-million-year-old skeleton found in Ethiopia. Many believe that humans and African apes share a common ancestor because of many of the features of these earliest remains.

LOOK UNDER THE FOLLOWING SUBJECTS IN THE LIBRARY CATALOG

Cave Dwellers
Cro-Magnons
Human Origins
Prehistoric Man

BROWSE FOR BOOKS ON THE SHELF USING THESE CALL NUMBERS

573.3 (Prehistoric Humankind)
930.1 (Archaeology)

REFERENCE MATERIALS THAT MAY HELP (BOOKS OR CD-ROMS)

Branigan, Keith. *Stone Age People*. World Book, 1996.
Early Humans. Knopf, 1989. (CD-ROM)
Evolution of Man. Expert, 1998.
Hawkes, Jacquetta. *The Atlas of Early Man*. St. Martin's Press, 1993.
Leakey, Richard. *The Origin of Humankind*. Basic Books, 1996.
Origins of Mankind. Maris, 1996. (CD-ROM)
Perdrizet, Marie-Pierre and Daniel Henon. *Prehistoric Life*. Raintree/Steck-Vaughn, 1990.

PERIODICAL INDEXES

EBSCO Magazine Article Summaries
InfoTrac
Reader's Guide to Periodical Literature

SUGGESTED INTERNET SITES

http://www.culture.fr/culture/arcnat/chauvet/en/gvpda-d.htm (The Chauvet Cave: the cave, the datings, the study, links)
http://users.hol.gr/~dilos/prehis.htm (Human prehistory: an exhibition)
http://www.emi.net/~bs-soft/Cro-Magnon.html (Cro-Magnon Man—discussion and links)

KEY WORDS FOR PERIODICAL AND ONLINE SEARCHES

Cave Dwellers
Fossil Man
Human Evolution
Prehistoric Man

VIDEO PROGRAMS RELATED TO THIS TOPIC

Paleoworld: Tracing Human Origins (3 video series). Ambrose Video, 1998.
Prehistoric Life. DK, 1996.

ORGANIZATIONS TO CONTACT FOR ADDITIONAL INFORMATION

American Anthropological Association, 4350 North Fairfax Drive, Suite 640, Arlington, VA 22203–1620. Phone: 703–528–1902, Fax: 703–528–3546.

Leakey Foundation, PO Box 29346, Presidio Building 1002A, O'Reilly Avenue, San Francisco, CA 94129–9911. Phone: 415–561–4646, Fax: 415–561–4647.

SUGGESTIONS FOR NARROWING THIS TOPIC

Compare and contrast Cro-Magnon man and the Neanderthal.

Create an annotated timeline illustrating geologic eras and periods during the history of mankind.

Discuss the findings in the Chauvet Cave, especially with regards to the significance of the discoveries and the methods of verification.

Relate how early man progressed from food gathering to more advanced ways of life.

RELATED TOPICS

Catastrophism
Creationism
Dinosaurs
Evolution

This RESEARCH TOPIC GUIDE is intended to help you find information on your topic in a wide variety of sources in this and any other library. Resources, though, are not limited to those described and not all libraries will have the same titles. Please ask a librarian for further guidance.

Reconstruction Period

BACKGROUND

Reconstruction was a period following the Civil War from 1865 to approximately 1898 during which the Union restored relations with the Southern States.

LOOK UNDER THE FOLLOWING SUBJECTS IN THE LIBRARY CATALOG

Reconstruction (1865–1876)

United States—History—1865–1898

BROWSE FOR BOOKS ON THE SHELF USING THIS CALL NUMBER

973.8 (Reconstruction Period, 1865–1901)

REFERENCE MATERIALS THAT MAY HELP (BOOKS OR CD-ROMS)

American Eras: Civil War and Reconstruction, 1850–1877. Gale Research, 1997.

DISCovering U.S. History. Gale Research, 1997. (CD-ROM)

Foner, Eric. *Reconstruction: America's Unfinished Revolution, 1863–1877.* Harper and Row, 1988.

Reconstruction. Clearvue/eav, 1994. (CD-ROM)

Richter, William L. *American Reconstruction 1862–1877.* ABC-CLIO, 1996.

PERIODICAL INDEXES

EBSCO Magazine Article Summaries

Index to *American Heritage* Magazine

InfoTrac

Reader's Guide to Periodical Literature

SUGGESTED INTERNET SITES

http://www.historychannel.com (Links to U.S. history through the 19th century)

http://www.umdl.umich.edu/moa/index.html (Making of America: A digital library of primary sources in social history from the Antebellum period through Reconstruction)

http://history.hanover.edu/19th/reconst.htm (Reconstruction and the "new South": links to texts and archives)

KEY WORDS FOR PERIODICAL AND ONLINE SEARCHES

Reconstruction
Reconstruction (Civil War)
United States—History—1865–1898

VIDEO PROGRAMS RELATED TO THIS TOPIC

The Geography of Hope. PBS, 1996.
Postwar Period. Coronet, 1983.
Reconstruction and Segregation. Schlessinger, 1996.

SUGGESTIONS FOR NARROWING THIS TOPIC

Discuss the 13th, 14th, and 15th Amendments to the Constitution.
Discuss issues of segregation after the Civil War.
Research life in the Southern States during the Reconstruction period.

RELATED TOPICS

Antebellum Life
Ku Klux Klan
Slavery
Underground Railroad

This RESEARCH TOPIC GUIDE is intended to help you find information on your topic in a wide variety of sources in this and any other library. Resources, though, are not limited to those described and not all libraries will have the same titles. Please ask a librarian for further guidance.

Rome, Ancient

BACKGROUND

The city of Rome was once the capital of the Roman Empire, which included millions of people who were united by the military and government of the Romans. We are still influenced today by the many contributions that the Romans made in government, the arts and architecture, technology, and literature.

LOOK UNDER THE FOLLOWING SUBJECTS IN THE LIBRARY CATALOG

Rome
Rome—Description
Rome—Geography

BROWSE FOR BOOKS ON THE SHELF USING THESE CALL NUMBERS

913.7 (Roman Empire—Description and Geography)
937 (Roman Empire)

REFERENCE MATERIALS THAT MAY HELP (BOOKS OR CD-ROMS)

Adkins, Lesley and Roy A. Adkins. *Handbook to Life in Ancient Rome.* Facts on File, 1994.
Ancient Civilizations: Greece and Rome. National Geographic, 1996. (CD-ROM)
Bunson, Matthew. *Encyclopedia of the Roman Empire.* Facts on File, 1994.
Chrisp, Peter. *The Roman Empire.* World Book, 1996.
Corbishley, Mike. *Ancient Rome.* Facts on File, 1989.
DISCovering World History. Gale Research, 1997. (CD-ROM)

PERIODICAL INDEXES

EBSCO Magazine Article Summaries
Index to *History Today* Magazine
InfoTrac
Reader's Guide to Periodical Literature

SUGGESTED INTERNET SITES

http://library.advanced.org/10098/rome.htm (Rome: past and present: From *Architecture through the Ages*)
http://history.evansville.net/rome.html (The Development of Western Civilization: World History: Rome—history, art, literature, music, mythology, etc.)

http://www.omnibusol.com/ancient.html (The Amazing Ancient World: An Internet journey weaving together people and civilizations)

KEY WORDS FOR PERIODICAL AND ONLINE SEARCHES

Ancient Civilizations
Ancient Rome
Rome

VIDEO PROGRAMS RELATED TO THIS TOPIC

History of Roman Civilization. Educational Video Network, 1988.
Roman City. PBS Video, 1994.
Rome: The Eternal City. Museum TV Workshop, 1994.
Rome: The Ultimate Empire. Time-Life Video, 1995.
Rome and Pompeii. Questar Video Communications, 1995.

SUGGESTIONS FOR NARROWING THIS TOPIC

Create an annotated timeline illustrating significant events of Ancient Roman history.

Discuss the role of women in Ancient Rome.

Research one of the following aspects of Ancient Rome: architecture, art, clothing, daily life, education, entertainment, literature, religion, or slavery.

RELATED TOPICS

Ancient Egypt
Ancient Greece

This RESEARCH TOPIC GUIDE is intended to help you find information on your topic in a wide variety of sources in this and any other library. Resources, though, are not limited to those described and not all libraries will have the same titles. Please ask a librarian for further guidance.

Slavery

BACKGROUND

Slavery is the forced labor and ownership of one human being by another. Slavery has been practiced throughout human history, existing even today in some parts of the world.

LOOK UNDER THE FOLLOWING SUBJECTS IN THE LIBRARY CATALOG

African Americans

Slavery

Slaves

Southern States—History

Underground Railroad

BROWSE FOR BOOKS ON THE SHELF USING THESE CALL NUMBERS

305.5 (Slaves)

306.3 (Economics Institutions, that is, slavery)

326 (Slavery and Emancipation)

973.7 (United States History, Civil War)

REFERENCE MATERIALS THAT MAY HELP (BOOKS OR CD-ROMS)

African-American History: Slavery to Civil Rights. Queue, 1996. (CD-ROM)

African American Voices of Triumph. Time-Life Books, 1995.

Altman, Susan. *The Encyclopedia of African-American Heritage.* Facts on File, 1997.

DISCovering U.S. History. Gale Research, 1997. (CD-ROM)

Hornsby, Alton, Jr. *Chronology of African American History. From 1492 to the Present.* Gale Research, 1997.

Miller, Randall and John David Smith, eds. *Dictionary of Afro-American Slavery.* Greenwood, 1997.

Rodriguez, Junius P., ed. *The Historical Encyclopedia of World Slavery.* ABC-CLIO, 1997.

PERIODICAL INDEXES

EBSCO Magazine Article Summaries

Index to *American Heritage* Magazine

InfoTrac

Reader's Guide to Periodical Literature

SUGGESTED INTERNET SITES

http://157.182.12.132/omdp/lesley/htm/abolits.htm (Short facts about abolitionists) http://sunsite.unc.edu/docsouth/ (University of North Carolina at Chapel Hill Library: Documentary of the American South: A full-text database of primary sources on Southern literature, including slave narratives)

http://www.nps.gov/undergroundrr/contents.htm (Underground railroad: Special resources study)

http://etext.lib.virginia.edu/rbs/rbsl6-95.html (African American Slavery—links, narratives, writings)

KEY WORDS FOR PERIODICAL AND ONLINE SEARCHES
Abolitionists
Slave Trade
Slavery
Underground Railroad

VIDEO PROGRAMS RELATED TO THIS TOPIC
The Amistad Revolt: All We Want Is Make Us Free. The Amistad Committee, 1995.
Death Runs Riot. PBS, 1996.
A History of Slavery in America. Schlessinger, 1994.
Roots of Resistance. WGBH-TV, 1990.

ORGANIZATION TO CONTACT FOR ADDITIONAL INFORMATION
Amnesty International. http://www.admin-us@aiusa.org

SUGGESTIONS FOR NARROWING THIS TOPIC
Debate the question: "Should the United States Government apologize for slavery, and if so, to whom?"
Discuss the economic aspects of slavery.
Discuss the Fugitive Slave Act of 1850.
Discuss slavery in other parts of the world than the United States and/or time period.

RELATED TOPICS
Apartheid
Civil Rights Movement
Racism
Reconstruction

This RESEARCH TOPIC GUIDE is intended to help you find information on your topic in a wide variety of sources in this and any other library. Resources, though, are not limited to those described and not all libraries will have the same titles. Please ask a librarian for further guidance.

Stock Market

BACKGROUND

Stock is a piece of ownership in a corporation. People who buy stock are called stockholders, and they own a part of the corporation of which they hold stock. The Stock Market is a system of organizations, linking businesses and investors all over the world, by which investors can buy stock.

LOOK UNDER THE FOLLOWING SUBJECTS IN THE LIBRARY CATALOG

Bonds
Investments
Stock Exchange
Wall Street (New York, N.Y.)

BROWSE FOR BOOKS ON THE SHELF USING THESE CALL NUMBERS

332.6–332.64 (Investment and Investments)

REFERENCE MATERIALS THAT MAY HELP (BOOKS OR CD-ROMS)

Bradley, Edward S. and Richard J. Teweles. *Stock Market*. John Wiley & Sons, 1998.

Dalton, John M. *How the Stock Market Works*. Prentice Hall, 1993.

Encarta. Microsoft. (CD-ROM Encyclopedia)

Grolier's Multimedia Encyclopedia. Grolier Interactive. (CD-ROM Encyclopedia)

Pool, John Charles and Robert L. Frick. *Demystifying the Stock Market*. Shenandoah University, 1994.

Young, Robin R. *The Stock Market*. Lerner, 1991.

PERIODICAL INDEXES

EBSCO Magazine Article Summaries
InfoTrac
Reader's Guide to Periodical Literature

SUGGESTED INTERNET SITES

http://cnnfn.com/markets/crash (Black Monday: A look back at the 1987 crash—CNN special report)

http://www.nasdaq.com (The Nasdaq Stock Market home page)

http://tqd.advanced.org/3088/ (Edu Stock: An educational web page designed to teach young and old alike what the Stock Market is and how it can work for them)

http://www.nyse.com (The New York Stock Exchange home page)

KEY WORDS FOR PERIODICAL AND ONLINE SEARCHES

American Stock Exchange
Nasdaq
New York Stock Exchange
Stock Market
Stocks

VIDEO PROGRAMS RELATED TO THIS TOPIC

Demystifying the Stock Market. Tapeworm Video, 1995.
A History of the Dow. Wall Street Journal, 1996.
Stock Market. ICA, 1998.
Stock Market: Investigate Before You Invest. National Geographic, 1998.

ORGANIZATION TO CONTACT FOR ADDITIONAL INFORMATION

New York Stock Exchange, 11 Wall Street, New York, NY 10005. Phone: 212–656–3000.

SUGGESTIONS FOR NARROWING THIS TOPIC

Choose a company and follow its stock for a month.
Discuss the differences between common stock and preferred stock.
Explain how the SEC (Securities Exchange Commission) protects brokers and investors.
Create a flowchart to illustrate to illustrate the steps involved in buying and selling stock.
Explain what a stock is and describe the four levels of stocks.

RELATED TOPICS

Business Ethics
Corporations
Credit Cards
Great Depression

This RESEARCH TOPIC GUIDE is intended to help you find information on your topic in a wide variety of sources in this and any other library. Resources, though, are not limited to those described and not all libraries will have the same titles. Please ask a librarian for further guidance.

Supreme Court

BACKGROUND

The highest court of the land is the Supreme Court, provided for in the Constitution of the United States under Article III.

LOOK UNDER THE FOLLOWING SUBJECT IN THE LIBRARY CATALOG

United States Supreme Court

BROWSE FOR BOOKS ON THE SHELF USING THIS CALL NUMBER

347.73 (Civil Procedure in the U.S.)

REFERENCE MATERIALS THAT MAY HELP (BOOKS OR CD-ROMS)

DISCovering U.S. History. Gale Research, 1997. (CD-ROM)

Jost, Kenneth. *The Supreme Court Yearbook*. Congressional Quarterly, date varies.

McGum, Barrett. *America's Court: The Supreme Court and the People*. Fulcrum Press, 1997.

Schwartz, Bernard. *A History of the Supreme Court*. Oxford University Press, 1995.

The U.S. Constitution and Supreme Court. Primary Source Media, 1997. (CD-ROM)

The United States Supreme Court. Grolier, 1995.

PERIODICAL INDEXES

EBSCO Magazine Article Summaries

Index to *American Heritage* Magazine

InfoTrac

Reader's Guide to Periodical Literature

SUGGESTED INTERNET SITES

http://supct.law.cornell.edu/supct/ (Archives of all Supreme Court opinions issued since May of 1990, from Cornell University)

http://www.fedworld.gov/supcourt/index.htm (Supreme Court decisions, 1937–1975)

http://supct.law.cornell.edu/supct/cases/historic.htm (Selected historic decisions of the U.S. Supreme Court, from Cornell University)

http://www.courttv.com/library/supreme (Court TV legal documents: The Supreme Court, famous cases)

KEY WORDS FOR PERIODICAL AND ONLINE SEARCHES

Civil Procedure
Legal System
Supreme Court
United States. Supreme Court

VIDEO PROGRAMS RELATED TO THIS TOPIC

Interpreting the Law: The Role of the Supreme Court. Guidance Associates, 1990.

The Supreme Court. Rainbow, 1993.

The Supreme Court in American Life: *A History*. Multi-Media Productions, 1990.

ORGANIZATION TO CONTACT FOR ADDITIONAL INFORMATION

The Supreme Court Historical Society, 111 Second Street, NE, Washington, DC 20002. Phone: 202–543–0400.

SUGGESTIONS FOR NARROWING THIS TOPIC

Discuss an historic Supreme Court case in terms of how the decision has affected society.

Discuss the style and most important decisions of a past or present Supreme Court Justice.

Trace the history of a Supreme Court case through the lower courts and summarize the Supreme Court decision.

Explain how a person gets appointed as Justice to the U.S. Supreme Court.

RELATED TOPICS

The Jury System
The Presidency

This RESEARCH TOPIC GUIDE is intended to help you find information on your topic in a wide variety of sources in this and any other library. Resources, though, are not limited to those described and not all libraries will have the same titles. Please ask a librarian for further guidance.

United States Civil War

BACKGROUND

The American Civil War, or War Between the States, began in 1861 with the Union Army attack on Fort Sumter in the harbor of Charleston. It ended in April of 1865, after four long, bloody years during which much of the South was brought to ruin. The end of the Civil War brought an end to slavery and settled the question of a state's right to secede from the Union.

LOOK UNDER THE FOLLOWING SUBJECTS IN THE LIBRARY CATALOG

Confederate States of America
Slavery—United States
United States—History—1861–1865, Civil War

BROWSE FOR BOOKS ON THE SHELF USING THIS CALL NUMBER

973.7 (U.S. Civil War)

REFERENCE MATERIALS THAT MAY HELP (BOOKS OR CD-ROMS)

American History: The Civil War. Byron Preiss Multimedia, 1995. (CD-ROM)

Batty, Peter Parish. *The Divided Union: The Story of the Great American War, 1861–1865.* Salem House, 1987.

The Civil War: Two Views. Clearvue/eav, 1994. (CD-ROM)

Davis, William C. *Commanders of the Civil War.* Salamander Books, 1990.

DISCovering U.S. History. Gale Research, 1997. (CD-ROM)

Goley, Michael. *The Civil War.* Facts on File, 1992.

PERIODICAL INDEXES

EBSCO Magazine Article Summaries
Index to *American Heritage* Magazine
InfoTrac
Reader's Guide to Periodical Literature

SUGGESTED INTERNET SITES

http://sunsite.utk.edu/civil-war (The American Civil War home page)

http://www.powerweb.net/bbock/war/ (Civil War medicine—links, bibliography)

http://www.historyplace.com/civilwar/index.html (The History Place: U.S. Civil War) http://www.uscivilwar.com/uscwhp2.cfm (U.S. Civil War: An interactive living history adventury)

KEY WORDS FOR PERIODICAL AND ONLINE SEARCHES

Civil War

United States—History—Civil War, 1861–1865

VIDEO PROGRAMS RELATED TO THIS TOPIC

Causes of the Civil War. Schlessinger, 1996.

The Civil War. Schlessinger, 1996.

The Massachusetts 54th Colored Infantry. PBS Video, 1991.

ORGANIZATION TO CONTACT FOR ADDITIONAL INFORMATION

The Civil War Society, PO Box 770, Berryville, VA 22611. Phone: 1–800–247–6253.

SUGGESTIONS FOR NARROWING THIS TOPIC

Create a fictional diary of a month in the life of either a Union or Confederate soldier.

Create an annotated timeline illustrating major events and battles of the Civil War.

Discuss the hardships suffered by the Southern people as the Civil War drew to a close.

Research the major causes of the Civil War.

RELATED TOPICS

The Confederacy

Plantation Life

Reconstruction

This RESEARCH TOPIC GUIDE is intended to help you find information on your topic in a wide variety of sources in this and any other library. Resources, though, are not limited to those described and not all libraries will have the same titles. Please ask a librarian for further guidance.

War of 1812

BACKGROUND

Disputes between the British and Americans over boundaries and shipping rights were primary causes of the War of 1812.

LOOK UNDER THE FOLLOWING SUBJECT IN THE LIBRARY CATALOG

United States—History—1812–1815, War of 1812

BROWSE FOR BOOKS ON THE SHELF USING THIS CALL NUMBER

973.5 (U.S. History—1809–1845)

REFERENCE MATERIALS THAT MAY HELP (BOOKS OR CD-ROMS)

Carter, Alden R. *The War of 1812: Second Fight for Independence*. Franklin Watts, 1992.

DISCovering U.S. History. Gale Research, 1997. (CD-ROM)

Encyclopedia of the War of 1812. ABC-CLIO, 1997.

Greenblat, Miriam. *The War of 1812*. Facts on File, 1994.

Marrin, Albert. *1812, The War Nobody Won*. Atheneum, 1985.

Nardo, Don. *The War of 1812*. Lucent Books, 1991.

Scribner American History and Culture. Scribner, 1998. (CD-ROM)

PERIODICAL INDEXES

EBSCO Magazine Article Summaries

Index to *American Heritage* Magazine

InfoTrac

Reader's Guide to Periodical Literature

SUGGESTED INTERNET SITES

http://alpha.binatech.on.ca/~bhmchin/ (Battlefield House Museum—Stoney Creek: location of the Battle of Stoney Creek during War of 1812)

http://www.bcpl.net/~etowner/patriot.html (Fort McHenry home page)

http://gateway.tippecanoe.com/tec_hist.html (History of Tecumseh and Tippecanoe)

http://home.earthlink.net/~gfeldmeth/chart.1812.html (Key events and causes: War of 1812)

KEY WORDS FOR PERIODICAL AND ONLINE SEARCHES

United States—History—War of 1812

United States—19th Century

War of 1812

VIDEO PROGRAMS RELATED TO THIS TOPIC

The Defense of Fort McHenry. National Parks Service.
Expansionism. Schlessinger, 1996.
The War of 1812. Coronet, 1982.
The War of 1812. ICA, 1994.

SUGGESTIONS FOR NARROWING THIS TOPIC

Create an annotated timeline illustrating significant battles and major events of the War of 1812.

Research the causes of the War of 1812.

Research the history behind the writing of the song *The Star Spangled Banner.*

Research the results and consequences of the War of 1812.

RELATED TOPICS

Revolutionary War
U.S. Flag
Westward Expansion

This RESEARCH TOPIC GUIDE is intended to help you find information on your topic in a wide variety of sources in this and any other library. Resources, though, are not limited to those described and not all libraries will have the same titles. Please ask a librarian for further guidance.

Westward Movement (U.S.)

BACKGROUND

The westward movement in the United States began in the 1600s when the early colonists began to move westward away from the Jamestown settlement and lasted until the late 1890s when all of the frontier had finally been conquered.

LOOK UNDER THE FOLLOWING SUBJECTS IN THE LIBRARY CATALOG

Oregon Trail
Overland Journeys to the Pacific
United States—Exploration
West (U.S.)

BROWSE FOR BOOKS ON THE SHELF USING THIS CALL NUMBER

978 (United States West)

REFERENCE MATERIALS THAT MAY HELP (BOOKS OR CD-ROMS)

The American West. World Book, 1997.
DISCovering U.S. History. Gale Research, 1997. (CD-ROM)
Jones, Mary Ellen. *Daily Life on the Nineteenth Century American Frontier*. Greenwood, 1998.
Freedman, Russell. *Children of the Wild West*. Clarion Books, 1983.
Matthews, Leonard J. *Pioneers*. Rourke, 1989.
Moss, Joyce. *Profiles in American History: Westward Movement to the Civil War*. U.X.L., 1994.

PERIODICAL INDEXES

EBSCO Magazine Article Summaries
Index to *American Heritage* Magazine
InfoTrac
Reader's Guide to Periodical Literature

SUGGESTED INTERNET SITES

http://www.americanwest.com/ (America's West: Development and History)
http://www.goldrush1849.com/ (California's Gold Rush Country: History sites)
http://www.heard.org/ (The Heard Museum: Native cultures and art)
http://www.ukans.edu/kansas/seneca/oregon/index.html (Oregon Trail: the Trail West)

KEY WORDS FOR PERIODICAL AND ONLINE SEARCHES

Frontier and Pioneer Life
Homesteading

Land Rushes
Westward Movement

VIDEO PROGRAMS RELATED TO THIS TOPIC

America's Historic Trails. Questar, 1997.

America's Westward Expansion. Knowledge Unlimited, 1996.

Best of the Real West (5 video programs). Arts and Entertainment, 1993.

Black West. Turner Home Entertainment, 1994.

The West (9 video programs). PBS/Turner, 1996.

ORGANIZATIONS TO CONTACT FOR ADDITIONAL INFORMATION

Branch of Long Distance Trails, National Park Service, Southwest Regional Office, PO Box 728, Santa Fe, NM 87504–0728.

Oregon-California Trails Association, PO Box 1019, Independence, MO 64051–0519. Phone: 816–252–2276, Fax: 816–836–0989.

SUGGESTIONS FOR NARROWING THIS TOPIC

Indicate on a U.S. map the routes of the following: the Chisholm Trail, the Oregon Trail, and the Santa Fe Trail.

Research the lives and contributions to America of one of the following pioneers/frontiersmen: Daniel Boone, Jim Bridger, Kit Carson, or Davy Crockett.

Research the California Gold Rush and the impact it had upon the settlement of the West.

Research the story of the Donner Pass.

RELATED TOPICS

Fur Trade
The Indian Wars
The Louisiana Purchase
Pony Express

This RESEARCH TOPIC GUIDE is intended to help you find information on your topic in a wide variety of sources in this and any other library. Resources, though, are not limited to those described and not all libraries will have the same titles. Please ask a librarian for further guidance.

IV

Social Issues

Apartheid

BACKGROUND

Apartheid in South Africa was both a racial ideology and a legal system under which Afrikaners (the white Dutch settlers) forced the Africans (blacks) to live under a system of laws that required the Africans to carry passbooks, restricted them to certain jobs, barred them from public facilities, prohibited them from voting, and banned interracial marriages. This white supremacy rule existed in South Africa from 1948 until 1994.

LOOK UNDER THE FOLLOWING SUBJECTS IN THE LIBRARY CATALOG

Apartheid
Segregation
South Africa—Race Relations

BROWSE FOR BOOKS ON THE SHELF USING THESE CALL NUMBERS

305.8 (Racial, Ethnic, National Groups)
320.5 (Political Ideologies)
968 (Republic of South Africa)

REFERENCE MATERIALS THAT MAY HELP (BOOKS OR CD-ROMS)

Berry, Ian and Chris Boot. *Living Apart: South Africa under Apartheid.* Phaidon, 1996.

DISCovering World History. Gale Research, 1997. (CD-ROM)

Eades, Lindsay M. *The End of Apartheid in South Africa.* Greenwood, 1999.

The Last Days of Apartheid. Society for Visual Education, 1996. (CD-ROM)

McSharry, Patra, Hugh Lewin, and Roger Rosen. *Apartheid: Calibrations of Color.* Rosen, 1991.

Pascoe, Elaine. *South Africa—Troubled Land.* Facts on File, 1992.

Waldmeir, Patti. *Anatomy of a Miracle: The End of Apartheid and the New South Africa.* W. W. Norton, 1997.

PERIODICAL INDEXES

EBSCO Magazine Article Summaries
InfoTrac
Reader's Guide to Periodical Literature

SUGGESTED INTERNET SITES

http://www.truth.org.za/ (Official home page: Truth and Reconciliation Commission) http://www.anc.org.za/ (Home Page: African National Congress)

http://www.sth-africa.com (South Africa: Official South African site on the web)

KEY WORDS FOR PERIODICAL AND ONLINE SEARCHES

Apartheid—South Africa

Blacks—South Africa

Mandela, Nelson

South Africa—Politics and Government

VIDEO PROGRAMS RELATED TO THIS TOPIC

Cry, the Beloved Country. Miramax, 1995.

Defiance in the Townships: Apartheid. Society for Visual Education, 1997.

Mandela and De Klerk. Showtime, 1997.

Mandela's Fight for Freedom. BBC/Discovery Channel, 1995.

They Come in Peace: A New Democratic South Africa. United Learning, 1994.

ORGANIZATION TO CONTACT FOR ADDITIONAL INFORMATION

African National Congress, 51 Plein Street, Johannesburg, South Africa 2001. Phone: 011–330–7000, Fax: 011–336–0097.

SUGGESTIONS FOR NARROWING THIS TOPIC

Compare the anti-apartheid movement in South Africa with the Civil Rights Movement in the United States.

Create an annotated timeline illustrating significant events and people during the system of apartheid in South Africa.

Research Nelson Mandela's role in the South African struggle against apartheid.

Research the main reasons for the eventual downfall of apartheid in South Africa.

RELATED TOPICS

Anti-semitism

Civil Rights Movement in the United States

Militia Movement in the United States

Racism

This RESEARCH TOPIC GUIDE is intended to help you find information on your topic in a wide variety of sources in this and any other library. Resources, though, are not limited to those described and not all libraries will have the same titles. Please ask a librarian for further guidance.

Cloning

BACKGROUND

In 1997, the birth of a sheep named Dolly made worldwide news because Dolly was a clone. Quickly the debate became intense over the ethics and morality of human cloning, now that it may be scientifically possible in the near future.

LOOK UNDER THE FOLLOWING SUBJECTS IN THE LIBRARY CATALOG

Clones and Cloning
Genetic Engineering
Molecular Cloning

BROWSE FOR BOOKS ON THE SHELF USING THESE CALL NUMBERS

174 (Medical Ethics)
575.1 (Genetics)
660 (Biotechnology)

REFERENCE MATERIALS THAT MAY HELP (BOOKS OR CD-ROMS)

Biology Explorer: Genetics. LOGAL Software. (CD-ROM)
Cohen, Daniel. *Cloning*. Millbrook Press, 1998.
DISCovering Science. Gale Research, 1997. (CD-ROM)
McGee, Glenn. *The Human Cloning Debate*. Berkeley Hills Books, 1998.
Reich, Warren T., ed. *Encyclopedia of Bioethics*. Macmillan Library Reference, 1995.
Winters, Paul A. *Cloning*. Greenhaven, 1998.

PERIODICAL INDEXES

EBSCO Magazine Article Summaries
InfoTrac
Reader's Guide to Periodical Literature
TOM Health and Science

SUGGESTED INTERNET SITES

http://www.cwrl.utexas.edu/~mchorost/e306/been/cloning.htm (Essay: "Can We and Should We Clone Humans?")
http://www.nimr.mrc.ac.uk/mhe97/cloning/htm (Essay on cloning from Mill Hill Essays 1997, National Institute for Medical Research)

KEY WORDS FOR PERIODICAL AND ONLINE SEARCHES

Bioethics

Cloning

Cloning—Moral and Ethical Aspects

Human Reproductive Technology

VIDEO PROGRAMS RELATED TO THIS TOPIC

Bioethics Forums. Videodiscovery, 1996.

Genes: The Language of Life. Lucerne Media, 1995.

Understanding Genetics: The Molecular Basis of Inheritance. United Learning, 1995.

ORGANIZATION TO CONTACT FOR ADDITIONAL INFORMATION

National Bioethics Advisory Commission, 6100 Executive Boulevard, Suite 5BOL, Rockville, MD 20892–7508. Phone: 301–402–4242, Fax: 301–480–6900.

SUGGESTIONS FOR NARROWING THIS TOPIC

Create and conduct a survey questioning a wide variety of people about their opinions of both animal and human cloning. Discuss your findings.

Research federal guidelines for human embryo cloning.

Research and debate the question: Should humans be cloned?

Research the history of cloning.

RELATED TOPICS

Bioethics

Cells

Genetics

Population Biology

This RESEARCH TOPIC GUIDE is intended to help you find information on your topic in a wide variety of sources in this and any other library. Resources, though, are not limited to those described and not all libraries will have the same titles. Please ask a librarian for further guidance.

Consumerism—Moral and Ethical Aspects

BACKGROUND

Twenty-five percent of the world's population consumes eighty percent of the world's material resources and owns over eighty percent of the wealth. Advertising helps businesses get the message about their products from them to us—the consumers. But, what messages are we sending our youth in terms of materialism? Everywhere we turn, we are being assaulted with advertising implying that our lives will be incomplete unless we have this or that item.

LOOK UNDER THE FOLLOWING SUBJECTS IN THE LIBRARY CATALOG

> Consumer Education
> Consumers
> Materialism

BROWSE FOR BOOKS ON THE SHELF USING THESE CALL NUMBERS

> 146 (Materialism)
> 640.73 (Consumer Education)
> 658.8 (Consumerism)
> 659.1 (Advertising)

REFERENCE MATERIALS THAT MAY HELP (BOOKS OR CD-ROMS)

> *Critical Thinking.* Compris. (CD-ROM)
> Frisch, Carlienne. *Hearing the Pitch: Evaluating All Kinds of Advertising.* Rosen, 1994.
> Key, Wilson B. *The Age of Manipulation: The Con in Confidence, The Sin in Sincere.* Madison Books, 1993.
> Mitchell, Susan. *Generation X: The Young Adult Market.* New Strategist, 1997.
> *Powers of Persuasion.* Fife and Drum, 1994. (CD-ROM)

PERIODICAL INDEXES

> *EBSCO Magazine Article Summaries*
> *InfoTrac*
> *Reader's Guide to Periodical Literature*

SUGGESTED INTERNET SITES

> http://www.enviroweb.org (Enviroweb)
> http://www.adbusters.org/main/index (Adbusters web page—fight consumerism)

http://www.utexas.edu/ftp/coc/adv/research/biblio/Subliminal.html (University of Texas, Dept. of Advertising: Advertising research)

KEY WORDS FOR PERIODICAL AND ONLINE SEARCHES
Advertising Ethics
Consumerism
Materialism

VIDEO PROGRAMS RELATED TO THIS TOPIC
Buy Me That Too! HBO, 1991.
Buy Me That 3! HBO, 1993.
Affluenza. Bullfrog Films, 1998.
Invisible Persuaders: The Battle for Your Mind. Learning Seed, 1994.

ORGANIZATIONS TO CONTACT FOR ADDITIONAL INFORMATION
The Contemporary Issues Agency, 1214 Coit Court, Waunakee, WI 53597. Phone: 608–849–6558.
The Media Foundation, 1243 West 7th Avenue, Vancouver, BC, V6H 1B7, Canada. Phone: 1–800–663–1243, Fax: 604–737–6021.

SUGGESTIONS FOR NARROWING THIS TOPIC
Discuss what individuals can do to raise human consciousness of the destructiveness of excessive consumerism.
Discuss how advertising encourages excessive consumerism.
Why did the major television networks reject the Buy Nothing Day advertisement in 1997?

RELATED TOPICS
Advertising
Mass Media

This RESEARCH TOPIC GUIDE is intended to help you find information on your topic in a wide variety of sources in this and any other library. Resources, though, are not limited to those described and not all libraries will have the same titles. Please ask a librarian for further guidance.

Divorce

BACKGROUND

Approximately 4.6 of every 1,000 Americans are divorced. Current statistics show that nearly half of all children will witness the breakup of their parents' marriage. Recently there have been movements nationwide for legislation to reduce divorce.

LOOK UNDER THE FOLLOWING SUBJECTS IN THE LIBRARY CATALOG

Divorce

Domestic Relations

BROWSE FOR BOOKS ON THE SHELF USING THESE CALL NUMBERS

173 (Ethics of Family Relationships, including Divorce)

306.89 (Separation and Divorce)

346.01 (Law of Domestic Relations)

REFERENCE MATERIALS THAT MAY HELP (BOOKS OR CD-ROMS)

The Encyclopedia of Social Issues. Marshall Cavendish, 1997.

Exploring Law and Society. Gale Research, 1998. (CD-ROM)

The Family: Opposing Viewpoints. Greenhaven, 1998.

Kronenwetter, Michael. *Encyclopedia of Modern American Social Issues*. ABC-CLIO, 1997.

Litten, W. Clark. *Family and the Law: A Dictionary*. ABC-CLIO, 1997.

Roleff, Tamara L. and Mary E. Williams. *Marriage and Divorce*. Greenhaven, 1997.

PERIODICAL INDEXES

EBSCO Magazine Article Summaries

InfoTrac

Reader's Guide to Periodical Literature

SUGGESTED INTERNET SITES

http://www.divorcesupport.com/ (The divorce support page: divorce, child custody, alimony, support, etc.)

http://www.divorce-online.com (Articles and information on various aspects of divorce)

http://patriot.net/~crouch/divorce.html (Divorce Reform page: information, opinions, and links about eforts to introduce laws to discourage and restrict divorce) http://www.divorcereform.org/ (Home page of Americans for Divorce Reform: links, information, and articles)

KEY WORDS FOR PERIODICAL AND ONLINE SEARCHES

Divorce

Divorce and Separation

Domestic Relations

Sociology—Marriage and Family

VIDEO PROGRAMS RELATED TO THIS TOPIC

Divorce. Coronet, 1981.

Divorce and the Family. Learning Seed, 1995.

Helping Children Cope with Divorce. Meridian Education, 1991.

Say Goodbye Again: Children of Divorce. Coronet/MTI, 1983.

ORGANIZATION TO CONTACT FOR ADDITIONAL INFORMATION

Americans for Divorce Reform, 2111 Wilson Boulevard, Suite 550, Arlinton, VA 22201–3057.

SUGGESTIONS FOR NARROWING THIS TOPIC

Discuss effects of divorce on children.

Discuss effects of divorce on society.

Discuss reasons for the increase in divorce in the last 30 years.

Discuss recent laws and legislation aimed at reducing divorce rates in the United States.

RELATED TOPICS

Domestic Violence

Family

Step Parents

Teenage Marriage

This RESEARCH TOPIC GUIDE is intended to help you find information on your topic in a wide variety of sources in this and any other library. Resources, though, are not limited to those described and not all libraries will have the same titles. Please ask a librarian for further guidance.

Education in the United States

BACKGROUND

The early colonists regarded education as a necessary process more for religious reasons than practical ones—one must be able to read so that the Bible could be studied. As early as 1647, Massachusetts passed a law requiring that towns of 50 or more population set up a school.

LOOK UNDER THE FOLLOWING SUBJECT IN THE LIBRARY CATALOG

Education—United States

BROWSE FOR BOOKS ON THE SHELF USING THIS CALL NUMBER

370.973 (Education—U.S.)

REFERENCE MATERIALS THAT MAY HELP (BOOKS OR CD-ROMS)

DISCovering U.S. History. Gale Research, 1997. (CD-ROM)

Eisenmann, Linda. *Historical Dictionary of Women's Education in the United States.* Greenwood, 1998.

Pulliam, John D. and James J. Van Patten. *History of Education in America.* Prentice Hall, 1998.

Spring, Joel H. *The American School, 1642–1996.* McGraw-Hill, 1997.

Webb, L. Dean, et al. *Foundations of American Education.* Macmillan, 1996.

PERIODICAL INDEXES

EBSCO Magazine Article Summaries
InfoTrac
Reader's Guide to Periodical Literature

SUGGESTED INTERNET SITES

http://lawlib.wuacc.edu/brown/brown.htm (Web site of *Brown v. Board of Education* Supreme Court case)

http://www.ed.gov/ (Home page of U.S. Department of Education)

http://edreform.com (Home page of the Center for Education Reform)

http://www.socsci.kun.nl/ped/whp/histeduc (The History of Education web site: International archive of links and source materials about history of education and childhood)

KEY WORDS FOR PERIODICAL AND ONLINE SEARCHES

Education—History
Education—United States

VIDEO PROGRAMS RELATED TO THIS TOPIC

The Endangered Teacher. Films for the Humanities and Sciences.
John Searle: What Should An Educated Person Know? Films for the Humanities and Sciences.

ORGANIZATION TO CONTACT FOR ADDITIONAL INFORMATION

U.S. Department of Education, 600 Independence Avenue, SW, Washington, DC 20202–0498. Phone: 1–800–US–LEARN.

SUGGESTIONS FOR NARROWING THIS TOPIC

Create an annotated timeline illustrating changing attitudes toward women's education throughout America's history.
Describe a typical day in a one-room schoolhouse of the 19th century.
Discuss characteristics of education in the original 13 colonies before 1776.
Discuss the influence of John Dewey on education.

RELATED TOPICS

Censorship
Copyright
History of Libraries
Literacy

This RESEARCH TOPIC GUIDE is intended to help you find information on your topic in a wide variety of sources in this and any other library. Resources, though, are not limited to those described and not all libraries will have the same titles. Please ask a librarian for further guidance.

Ethics and Morality

BACKGROUND

Moral issues include such topics as abortion, alcohol and drug abuse, adultery, pre-marital sex, etcetera. Many Americans feel that there is a moral decline in the United States today because there is a proliferation and acceptance of these conducts.

LOOK UNDER THE FOLLOWING SUBJECTS IN THE LIBRARY CATALOG

> Ethics
>
> Good and Evil
>
> Values

BROWSE FOR BOOKS ON THE SHELF USING THESE CALL NUMBERS

> 170 (Ethics and Moral Philosophy)
>
> 216 (Good and Evil)
>
> 241 (Moral Theology; Codes of Conduct)
>
> 303.3 (Values)

REFERENCE MATERIALS THAT MAY HELP (BOOKS OR CD-ROMS)

> *Encyclopedia of Bioethics, 2/e.* Macmillan Reference Library, 1996. (CD-ROM)
>
> *Ethics and Values* (5 volumes). Grolier Educational, 1999.
>
> Hester, Joseph P. *Encyclopedia of Values and Ethics*. ABC-CLIO, 1996.
>
> Kronenwetter, Michael. *Twentieth Century American Social Issues*. ABC-CLIO, 1997.
>
> Reich, Warren T. *Encyclopedia of Bioethics*. Macmillan Library Reference, 1995.

PERIODICAL INDEXES

> *EBSCO Magazine Article Summaries*
>
> *InfoTrac*
>
> *Reader's Guide to Periodical Literature*

SUGGESTED INTERNET SITES

> http://www.drlaura.com (The Official Dr. Laura Schlessinger web site)
>
> http://ethics.acusd.edu (Provides up-to-date information on current literature and internet links that relate to ethics)

KEY WORDS FOR PERIODICAL AND ONLINE SEARCHES

> Ethics
>
> Moral Values
>
> Morality
>
> Values

VIDEO PROGRAMS RELATED TO THIS TOPIC

Acting on Your Values. Coronet/MTI.

Alone in the Dark. Vision Video, 1994.

Ethics in America (5 video series). The Annenberg/CPB Collection, 1989.

Personal Ethics and the Future of the World. Varied Directions, 1991.

ORGANIZATIONS TO CONTACT FOR ADDITIONAL INFORMATION

Citizens for Community Values, 11175 Reading Road, Suite 103, Cincinnati, OH 45241. Phone: 513–733–5775.

The Society for Ethics, c/o Barbara J. Hall, Department of Philosophy, Georgia State University, Atlanta, GA 30303.

SUGGESTIONS FOR NARROWING THIS TOPIC

Debate: Does today's popular music contribute to the moral decline of today's youth?

Discuss what distinguishes or determines right from wrong?

How do moral issues affect society?

What do people mean by the phrase "traditional values?"

RELATED TOPICS

Philosophy

Religion

This RESEARCH TOPIC GUIDE is intended to help you find information on your topic in a wide variety of sources in this and any other library. Resources, though, are not limited to those described and not all libraries will have the same titles. Please ask a librarian for further guidance.

Euthanasia

BACKGROUND

Euthanasia is the practice of ending the life of an individual who is suffering from a terminal illness or an incurable condition. Euthanasia is usually carried out by either lethal injection or by the suspension of extraordinary treatment.

LOOK UNDER THE FOLLOWING SUBJECTS IN THE LIBRARY CATALOG

Euthanasia

Medical Ethics

Right to Die

BROWSE FOR BOOKS ON THE SHELF USING THESE CALL NUMBERS

174 (Medical Ethics)

179 (Euthanasia)

REFERENCE MATERIALS THAT MAY HELP (BOOKS OR CD-ROMS)

Encyclopedia of Bioethics, 2/e. Macmillan Library Reference, 1996. (CD-ROM)

Encyclopedia of Social Issues. Marshall Cavendish, 1997.

Exploring Law & Society. Gale Research, 1998.

Kronenwetter, Michael. *Encyclopedia of Modern American Social Issues.* ABC-CLIO, 1997.

Reich, Warren T., ed. *Encyclopedia of Bioethics.* Macmillan Library Reference, 1995.

Roberts, Carolyn S. and Martha Gorman. *Euthanasia.* ABC-CLIO, 1996.

PERIODICAL INDEXES

EBSCO Magazine Article Summaries

InfoTrac

Reader's Guide to Periodical Literature

SIRS (Social Issues Resources Series)

SUGGESTED INTERNET SITES

http://www.finalexit.org/ (Newstories, Right to Die Societies, Laws, Books, Movies, Essays, and more pertaining to euthanasia)

http://www.interlife.org/kevorkian (Articles, transcripts of speeches and interviews, legal documentation, related links—all pertaining to Dr. Kevorkian)

http://www.euthansia.com (Information for research on euthanasia, physician-assisted suicide, living wills, and mercy killing) http://www.kyrie.com/actrtla/euthan.htm (Anti-euthanasia articles from the ACT Right to Life Association)

KEY WORDS FOR PERIODICAL AND ONLINE SEARCHES

Assisted Suicide

Euthanasia

Right to Die

VIDEO PROGRAMS RELATED TO THIS TOPIC

Bioethics Forums. Videodiscovery, 1996.

Does Doctor Know Best? Annenberg/CPB Collection, 1989.

Last Wish. ABC TV, 1992.

Leon R. Kass: The Moral Implications of Scientific Advances. Films for the Humanities and Sciences, 1988.

ORGANIZATIONS TO CONTACT FOR ADDITIONAL INFORMATION

Euthanasia Research and Guidance Organization, 24829 Norris Lane, Junction City, OR 97448–9559. Fax: 541–998–1873.

Pro-Life Council, 190 Main Street, East Haven, CT 06512. Phone: 203–469–9185, Fax: 203–467–8602. rsmithpl@ix.netcom.com

SUGGESTIONS FOR NARROWING THIS TOPIC

Debate the pros and cons of euthanasia.

Discuss the differences between euthanasia and physician-assisted suicide.

Research the services of hospice care for the dying.

What is a living will?

RELATED TOPICS

Disease Prevention

Health Care Debate

Medical Trends

Transplantation

This RESEARCH TOPIC GUIDE is intended to help you find information on your topic in a wide variety of sources in this and any other library. Resources, though, are not limited to those described and not all libraries will have the same titles. Please ask a librarian for further guidance.

Food Safety

Almost daily there is a news report about an outbreak somewhere in the United States of a foodborne illness. Such illnesses can be caused by contamination of raw agricultural products, improper handling during food preparation, improper storage of foods, and more. Consumer education is essential in the move to decrease illnesses and deaths caused by food.

LOOK UNDER THE FOLLOWING SUBJECTS IN THE LIBRARY CATALOG

Edible Plants

Food Additives

Food Contamination

Food Poisoning

BROWSE FOR BOOKS ON THE SHELF USING THESE CALL NUMBERS

363.19 (Food Hazards)

664 (Food Preservation)

REFERENCE MATERIALS THAT MAY HELP (BOOKS OR CD-ROMS)

Goldstein, Joan. *Demanding Clean Food and Water: The Fight for a Basic Human Right.* Plenum, 1990.

McSwane, David, et al. *Essentials of Food Safety and Sanitation.* Prentice Hall, 1998.

Mayo Clinic Family Health. IVI, 1995. (CD-ROM)

Patten, Barbara J. *Food Safety.* The Rourke Book, 1997.

Scott, Elizabeth and Paul Sockett. *How to Prevent Food Poisoning: A Practical Guide to Safe Cooking, Eating, and Food Handling.* John Wiley & Sons, 1998.

PERIODICAL INDEXES

EBSCO Magazine Article Summaries

InfoTrac

Reader's Guide to Periodical Literature

TOM Health and Science

SUGGESTED INTERNET SITES

http://www.fsis.usda.gov (Home page of USDA Food Safety and Inspection Service—includes consumer information)

http://vm.cfsan.fda.gov/~mow/intro.html (A handbook from USDA providing basic facts regarding foodborne pathogenic microorganisms and natural toxins) http://www.fightbac.org (Fighting the problem of foodborne illness, from the Partnership for Food Safety Education)

KEY WORDS FOR PERIODICAL AND ONLINE SEARCHES
Food Contamination
Food Poisoning
Food Safety
Foodborne Diseases

VIDEO PROGRAMS RELATED TO THIS TOPIC
Food Safety: What You Don't Know Can Hurt You. Meka, 1996.
Food Safety Law. John Wiley & Sons, 1997.
Kitchen Food Safety for the Family. National Health, 1997.

ORGANIZATION TO CONTACT FOR ADDITIONAL INFORMATION
USDA Food Safety & Inspection Service, Room 1175—South Building, 1400 Independence Avenue, SW, Washington, DC 20250. Phone: 202–720–7943, Fax: 202–720–1843.

SUGGESTIONS FOR NARROWING THIS TOPIC
Create an annotated poster illustrating safe food handling procedures.
Discuss the causes and results of botulism.
Research four types of foodborne illnesses: bacterial, parasitic, viral, and toxin.
Research three recent outbreaks of foodborne illnesses.

RELATED TOPICS
Bacteria
Diseases

This RESEARCH TOPIC GUIDE is intended to help you find information on your topic in a wide variety of sources in this and any other library. Resources, though, are not limited to those described and not all libraries will have the same titles. Please ask a librarian for further guidance.

Gender Roles

BACKGROUND

Over the last ten or twenty years, America has undergone a dramatic change regarding gender roles. More women are working outside the home, necessitating men to assume many household duties once thought of as "women's work." At the same time, parents are demanding equal opportunities in school and sports for their daughters and women are demanding equal opportunities and equal pay in the workplace.

LOOK UNDER THE FOLLOWING SUBJECTS IN THE LIBRARY CATALOG

Role Conflict

Sex Differences

Sex Role

BROWSE FOR BOOKS ON THE SHELF USING THESE CALL NUMBERS

155.3 (Sex Psychology)

305.3 (Sex Role)

REFERENCE MATERIALS THAT MAY HELP (BOOKS OR CD-ROMS)

Beal, Carole R. *Boys and Girls: The Development of Gender Roles*. McGraw Hill, 1994.

Bender, David L. and Bruno Leone. *Male/Female Roles: Opposing Viewpoints*. Greenhaven, 1995.

Burke, Phyllis. *Gender Shock: Exploding the Myths of Male and Female*. Anchor, 1997.

Gray, John. *Men Are from Mars, Women Are from Venus*. HarperCollins, 1992.

Rudd, Peggy J. *Who's Really from Venus? The Tale of Two Genders*. PM Publishers, 1998.

Stearman, Kay and Nikki Van Der Gaag. *Gender Issues*. Thomson Learning, 1996.

PERIODICAL INDEXES

EBSCO Magazine Article Summaries

InfoTrac

Reader's Guide to Periodical Literature

SIRS (Social Issues Resources Series)

SUGGESTED INTERNET SITES

http://www.taiga.ca/~balance (A webzine that seeks to discuss gender issues and politics which are largely ignored by mainstream media)

http://www.washingtonpost.com/wp-srv/national/longterm/gender/gen-der22a.htm (Series of articles from the *Washington Post* on the gender revolution)

http://osu.orst.edu/~huj/512/ (Discussion of children's toys and gender)

http://www.cyberparent.com/gender/gender.htm (Genders and gender understanding in relationships)

KEY WORDS FOR PERIODICAL AND ONLINE SEARCHES
Gender Identity
Gender Psychology
Gender Roles
Sex Differences

VIDEO PROGRAMS RELATED TO THIS TOPIC
The Men's Movement. Films for the Humanities and Sciences.
Sex and Gender. WGBH/Boston for the Annenberg/CPB Project, 1989.
Woman's Place. View Video, 1983.

ORGANIZATION TO CONTACT FOR ADDITIONAL INFORMATION
Society for the Psychological Study of Men and Masculinity, Division 51, Administrative Office, c/o American Psychological Association, 750 1st Street, NE, Washington, DC 20002.

SUGGESTIONS FOR NARROWING THIS TOPIC
Discuss the pros and cons of single-sex education.
Do toys make a difference in children's gender identification?
How does society affect a person's concept of gender behavior?
Research changing roles of men and women in the 1990s.

RELATED TOPICS
Androgyny
Homosexuality
Sexism
Sexual Harassment

This RESEARCH TOPIC GUIDE is intended to help you find information on your topic in a wide variety of sources in this and any other library. Resources, though, are not limited to those described and not all libraries will have the same titles. Please ask a librarian for further guidance.

Marijuana, Legalization of

BACKGROUND

At a time when government leaders are pushing harder than ever for tougher drug laws, advocates for legalization of marijuana, especially for medicinal purposes, are also getting their message across.

LOOK UNDER THE FOLLOWING SUBJECTS IN THE LIBRARY CATALOG

> Drug Abuse
> Drug Therapy
> Drugs—Physiological Effect
> Marijuana
> Narcotics

BROWSE FOR BOOKS ON THE SHELF USING THESE CALL NUMBERS

> 362.29 (Substance Abuse)
> 615 (Therapeutics)

REFERENCE MATERIALS THAT MAY HELP (BOOKS OR CD-ROMS)

> Grinspoon, Lester. *Marihuana Reconsidered.* Quick Trading, 1994.
> Marshall, Eliot. *Legalization: A Debate.* Chelsea House, 1988.
> O'Brien, Robert, et al. *The Encyclopedia of Drug Abuse.* Facts on File, 1992.
> Terkel, Susan Neiburg. *The Drug Laws: A Time for Change?* Franklin Watts, 1997.
> *Understanding Alcohol and Other Drugs: A Multimedia Resource.* Facts on File, 1997. (CD-ROM)

PERIODICAL INDEXES

> *EBSCO Magazine Summaries*
> *InfoTrac*
> *Reader's Guide to Periodical Literature*
> *SIRS (Social Issues Resources Series)*

SUGGESTED INTERNET SITES

> http://www.mpp.org/ (Home page of the Marijuana Policy Project; includes legislative updates)
> http://www.drugnet.org/orgs/dsi (Non-profit information network and advocacy organization promoting the creation of drug-free culture and opposing the legalization of drugs)

http://www.nida.nih.gov/MarijBroch/Marijintro.html (National Institute on Drug Abuse brochures with facts about marijuana for teens and for parents)

KEY WORDS FOR PERIODICAL AND ONLINE SEARCHES

Legalization of Marijuana

Marijuana

VIDEO PROGRAMS RELATED TO THIS TOPIC

Hard Facts about Drugs: Alcohol. Marijuana, Cocaine, and Crack. Guidance Associates, 1988.

Marijuana: Its Effects on Mind and Body. Schlessinger Video, 1991.

Prescription Narcotics: The Addictive Painkiller. Schlessinger Video, 1991.

What's Wrong with Marijuana? Human Relations Media, 1995.

ORGANIZATIONS TO CONTACT FOR ADDITIONAL INFORMATION

Marijuana Policy Project, PO Box 77492, Washington, DC 20013.

National Institute on Drug Abuse. http://www.nida.nih.gov

SUGGESTIONS FOR NARROWING THIS TOPIC

Discuss the social implications if marijuana were legalized.

Research arguments for and against legalization of marijuana.

Research recent proposed legislation regarding the legalization of marijuana, both at state and national levels.

RELATED TOPICS

Barbiturates

Nicotine

Painkillers

Prescription Drugs

This RESEARCH TOPIC GUIDE is intended to help you find information on your topic in a wide variety of sources in this and any other library. Resources, though, are not limited to those described and not all libraries will have the same titles. Please ask a librarian for further guidance.

Mental Illness

BACKGROUND

There are 292 disorders classified as mental illnesses (*U.S. News & World*, 1992). These disorders include minor depression and binge eating, as well as schizophrenia and manic-depression.

LOOK UNDER THE FOLLOWING SUBJECTS IN THE LIBRARY CATALOG

> Mental Health
> Mental Illness
> Mentally Ill

BROWSE FOR BOOKS ON THE SHELF USING THESE CALL NUMBERS

> 362.2 (Mental and Emotional Illnesses and Disturbances)
> 616.89 (Mental Disorders)

REFERENCE MATERIALS THAT MAY HELP (BOOKS OR CD-ROMS)

> Beins, Bernard, et al., eds. *The Gale Encyclopedia of Psychology*. Gale Research, 1996.
> Bender, David and Bruno Leone, eds. *Mental Illness: Opposing Viewpoints*. Greenhaven, 1995.
> Grob, Gerald N. *The Mad among Us: A History of the Care of America's Mentally Ill*. Belknap, 1995.
> Hales, Dianne and Robert E. Hales. *Caring for the Mind: The Comprehensive Guide to Mental Health*. Bantam Books, 1995.
> Hyde, Margaret O. and Elizabeth H. Forsyth. *Know about Mental Illness*. Walker & Co., 1996.
> Shorter, Edward. *A History of Psychiatry: From the Era of the Asylum to the Age of Prozac*. John Wiley & Sons, 1997.

PERIODICAL INDEXES

> *EBSCO Magazine Article Summaries*
> *InfoTrac*
> *Reader's Guide to Periodical Literature*
> *SIRS (Social Issues Resources Series)*

SUGGESTED INTERNET SITES

> http://www.mentalhealth.com (A free internet encyclopedia of mental health information)
> http://www.alz.org (Home page of the National Alzheimer's Association)
> http://www.sover.net/~schwcof (Web site offering information about Anxiety Disorders)

http://www.psy.med.rug.nl/0031 (Questions and answers about schizophrenia)

KEY WORDS FOR PERIODICAL AND ONLINE SEARCHES
Mental Health
Mental Illness
Mentally Ill
Also search under names of specific mental illnesses.

VIDEO PROGRAMS RELATED TO THIS TOPIC
Psychopathology. The Annenberg/CPB Project, 1989.
The World of Abnormal Psychology (13 video programs). Levine Communi-
cations, 1992.

ORGANIZATIONS TO CONTACT FOR ADDITIONAL
INFORMATION
Alzheimer's Association National Office, 919 North Michigan Avenue,
Suite 1000, Chicago, IL 60611–1676. Fax: 312–335–1110.
The Coalition of Voluntary Mental Health Agencies, Inc., 120 West 57 Street,
New York, NY 10019. Phone: 212–586–4555, Fax: 212–541–6183.

SUGGESTIONS FOR NARROWING THIS TOPIC
Compare treatment of the mentally ill fifty years ago with treatment today.
Discuss symptoms, causes, and treatments of one of the following anxiety dis-
orders: agoraphobia, obsessive compulsive disorder, or post-traumatic
stress disorder.
Research the warning signs of, progress of, and treatments available for alz-
heimer's disease.
Research treatment options for schizophrenia.

RELATED TOPICS
Addiction
Eating Disorders
Suicide
Violent Behavior

This RESEARCH TOPIC GUIDE is intended to help you find information on your topic in a
wide variety of sources in this and any other library. Resources, though, are not limited to
those described and not all libraries will have the same titles. Please ask a librarian for further
guidance.

Organ Transplantation

BACKGROUND

The many medical advances which make possible the successful transplantation of organs are useless if there are not enough people willing to become organ and tissue donors. The need for organs and tissue exceed supply. Public awareness and individual preparedness are essential factors if more lives are to be saved by this "gift of life."

LOOK UNDER THE FOLLOWING SUBJECTS IN THE LIBRARY CATALOG

Donation of Organs, Tissues, etcetera

Heart—Transplantation

Transplantation Organs, Tissues, etcetera

BROWSE FOR BOOKS ON THE SHELF USING THIS CALL NUMBER

617.9 (Transplantation of Organs)

REFERENCE MATERIALS THAT MAY HELP (BOOKS OR CD-ROMS)

Caplan, Arthur and Daniel H. Coelho, eds. *The Ethics of Organ Transplants: The Current Debate*. Prometheus Books, 1998.

DISCovering Science. Gale Research, 1997.

Durrett, Deanne. *Organ Transplants*. Lucent Books, 1993.

Encyclopedia of Bioethics, 2/e. Macmillan Library Reference, 1996. (CD-ROM)

Medical Discoveries: Medical Breakthroughs and the People Who Developed Them. U.X.L., 1997.

Reich, Warren T. *Encyclopedia of Bioethics*. Macmillan Library Reference, 1995.

PERIODICAL INDEXES

EBSCO Magazine Article Summaries

InfoTrac

Reader's Guide to Periodical Literature

SIRS (Social Issues Resources Series)

TOM Health and Science

SUGGESTED INTERNET SITES

http://www.wrtc.org (Questions and answers, links, brochure sources, and other facts about donation and transplantation of organs and tissue)

http://www.transweb.org/journey/index.html (A detailed "journey" about having a kidney transplant) http://www.transweb.org (A nonprofit educational Internet resource devoted to transplantation and donation)

http://www.mediconsult.com/liver/shareware/organtrans (Facts and figures about organ transplantation and donation)

KEY WORDS FOR PERIODICAL AND ONLINE SEARCHES

Donation of Organs, Tissues, etcetera

Transplantation of Organs, Tissues, etcetera

VIDEO PROGRAMS RELATED TO THIS TOPIC

Bone Marrow Transplants. Films for the Humanities and Sciences.

Receiving and Donating Organs. Films for the Humanities and Sciences.

Second Chance: Organ Transplants. Films for the Humanities and Sciences.

ORGANIZATIONS TO CONTACT FOR ADDITIONAL INFORMATION

Coalition on Donation, 1100 Boulders Parkway, Suite 500, Richmond, VA 23225. Phone: 804–327–1447, Fax: 804–323–7343.

TransWeb, The Northern Brewery Building, 1327 Jones Drive, Suite 105, Ann Arbor, MI 48105. Phone: 734–998–7314, Fax: 734–998–6710.

SUGGESTIONS FOR NARROWING THIS TOPIC

Create an annotated transplantation timeline illustrating major break-throughs in organ and tissue transplantation, beginning with the first successful cornea transplant in 1905.

Discuss ethical issues related to organ transplantation.

How is brain death determined?

Research xenotransplantation.

RELATED TOPICS

Cloning

Death and Dying

Euthanasia

This RESEARCH TOPIC GUIDE is intended to help you find information on your topic in a wide variety of sources in this and any other library. Resources, though, are not limited to those described and not all libraries will have the same titles. Please ask a librarian for further guidance.

Population Control

BACKGROUND

How many people are too many? And, if the world has too many people, what should be done about it? Population control is a controversial issue that involves religion, morality, politics, and more.

LOOK UNDER THE FOLLOWING SUBJECTS IN THE LIBRARY CATALOG

Birth Control
Family Planning
Human Ecology
Population Control

BROWSE FOR BOOKS ON THE SHELF USING THESE CALL NUMBERS

304.6 (Population)
363.9 (Population Problems)

REFERENCE MATERIALS THAT MAY HELP (BOOKS OR CD-ROMS)

Aaseng, Nathan. *Overpopulation: Crisis or Challenge*. Franklin Watts, 1991.
Bender, David L. and Bruno Leone. *Population: Opposing Viewpoints*. Greenhaven, 1995.
Cohen, Joel E. *How Many People Can the Earth Support?* W. W. Norton, 1996.
Ehrlich, Paul. *The Population Bomb*. Buccaneer Books, 1997.
Livi-Bacci, Massimo. *A Concise History of World Population*. Blackwell, 1997.
Winckler, Suzanne, et al. *Our Endangered Planet: Population Growth*. Lerner, 1991.

PERIODICAL INDEXES

EBSCO Magazine Article Summaries
InfoTrac
Reader's Guide to Periodical Literature
SIRS (Social Issues Resources Series)

SUGGESTED INTERNET SITES

http://www.pop.org (Home page of the Population Research Institute—articles, opinions, statistics, and links related to population)
http://www.popexpo.net (Discover the mechanism of population growth through a museum's interactive experience)

http://www.popnet.org/ (Global population information with links to hundreds of sources)

http://www.census.gov (The Official U.S. Census Bureau page—social, demographic, and economic information)

KEY WORDS FOR PERIODICAL AND ONLINE SEARCHES
Birth Control
Demography
Human Ecology
Population Control

VIDEO PROGRAMS RELATED TO THIS TOPIC
Jam Packed: The Challenge of Human Overpopulation. Video Project, 1997.
World War III: The Population Explosion and Our Planet. Video Project, 1995.

ORGANIZATION TO CONTACT FOR ADDITIONAL INFORMATION
Population Research Institute, 5119A Leesburg Pike, Suite 295, Falls Church, VA 22401. Phone: 540–622–5240.

SUGGESTIONS FOR NARROWING THIS TOPIC
Discuss problems caused by overpopulation in developing countries.
Research China's population control program.
Research human rights abuses resulting from population control.
Research recent U.S. legislative actions related to population control.

RELATED TOPICS
Environment
Food Supply
Pollution

This RESEARCH TOPIC GUIDE is intended to help you find information on your topic in a wide variety of sources in this and any other library. Resources, though, are not limited to those described and not all libraries will have the same titles. Please ask a librarian for further guidance.

Prayer in Schools

BACKGROUND

In 1962, the U.S. Supreme Court ruled, in the case of *Engel v. Vitale*, that it was unconstitutional for the state of New York to allow the recitation of prayer in their public schools. The following year, in the case of *Abington School District v. Schempp*, the practice of beginning the school day with a prayer or devotional Bible reading was prohibited. Since then, prayer in school has remained a controversy.

LOOK UNDER THE FOLLOWING SUBJECTS IN THE LIBRARY CATALOG

Church and State

Religion in the Public Schools

BROWSE FOR BOOKS ON THE SHELF USING THIS CALL NUMBER

377 (Schools and Religion)

REFERENCE MATERIALS THAT MAY HELP (BOOKS OR CD-ROMS)

Alley, Robert S. *School Prayer: The Court, the Congress, and the First Amendment*. Prometheus Books, 1994.

Andryszewski, Tricia. *School Prayer: A History of the Debate*. Enslow Publishers, 1997.

Constitution and Supreme Court. Primary Source, 1996. (CD-ROM)

DISCovering U.S. History. Gale Research, 1997. (CD-ROM)

Jurinski, James John. *Religion in the Schools*. ABC-CLIO, 1998.

Landmark Decisions of the United States Supreme Court I. Excellent Books, 1991.

Taylor, Bonnie B. *Education and the Law*. ABC-CLIO, 1997.

PERIODICAL INDEXES

EBSCO Magazine Article Summaries

InfoTrac

Reader's Guide to Periodical Literature

SIRS (Social Issues Resources Series)

SUGGESTED INTERNET SITES

http://www.softdisk.com/comp/shume/politics/pray1.html (Ten reasons for voluntary school prayer—editorial)

http://www.aclu.org/index.html (Home page of American Civil Liberties Union, where a search can be made of the organization's positions on school prayer)

http://www.atheists.org/courthouse/prayer.html (Commemorative reprint, with background information, of the Supreme Court's opinion on the subject) http://www.cwfa.org/policypapers/pp_prayer.html (School prayer and religious liberty: a Constitutional perspective)

KEY WORDS FOR PERIODICAL AND ONLINE SEARCHES

Prayer in Schools
Prayer in the Public Schools
Religion and Schools
School Prayer

VIDEO PROGRAM RELATED TO THIS TOPIC

School Prayer, Gun Control, & the Right to Assemble. The Annenberg/CPB Collection, 1984.

ORGANIZATIONS TO CONTACT FOR ADDITIONAL INFORMATION

American Civil Liberties Union, 125 Broad Street, New York, NY 10004–2400.

Concerned Women for America, 1015 Fifteenth Street, NW, Suite 1100, Washington, DC 20005. Phone: 202–488–7000, Fax: 202–488–0806.

SUGGESTIONS FOR NARROWING THIS TOPIC

Create an annotated timeline illustrating major legislation and court decisions regarding religion and public schools.

Discuss separation of church and state according to the Declaration of Independence and the Constitution of the United States.

Research background to the Supreme Court rulings in 1962 and 1963 which found official prayer in public schools to be unconstitutional.

RELATED TOPICS

Ethics and Morality
Religion and Society
School Violence
Supreme Court Decisions

This RESEARCH TOPIC GUIDE is intended to help you find information on your topic in a wide variety of sources in this and any other library. Resources, though, are not limited to those described and not all libraries will have the same titles. Please ask a librarian for further guidance.

Racism

BACKGROUND

Racism is discrimination or prejudice based on race—not on the qualities that another person possesses. Racists believe that race accounts for differences in human qualities or abilities and that one particular race is superior over others.

LOOK UNDER THE FOLLOWING SUBJECTS IN THE LIBRARY CATALOG

Prejudices
Race Relations
Racial Discrimination
Racism

BROWSE FOR BOOKS ON THE SHELF USING THESE CALL NUMBERS

177 (Ethics of Social Relations)
303.3 (Prejudice)
305.8 (Racial, Ethnic, National Groups)
320.5 (Political Ideologies)

REFERENCE MATERIALS THAT MAY HELP (BOOKS OR CD-ROMS)

Able, Deborah. *Hate Groups*. Enslow, 1995.
DISCovering Multicultural America. Gale Research, 1996.
Gay, Kathlyn. *I Am Who I Am: Speaking out about Multiracial Identity*. Franklin Watts, 1995.
Pascoe, Elaine. *Racial Prejudice: Why Can't We Overcome?* Franklin Watts, 1997.
Shaughnessy, Diane. *Let's Talk about Racism*. Powerkids, 1998.
Sheftel-Gomes, Nasoan. *Everything You Need to Know about Racism*. Rosen, 1998.

PERIODICAL INDEXES

EBSCO Magazine Article Summaries
InfoTrac
Reader's Guide to Periodical Literature
SIRS (Social Issues Resources Series)

SUGGESTED INTERNET SITES

http://www.ceousa.org (Home page of the Center for Equal Opportunity—includes articles and links) http://www.udayton.edu/~race/ (Race and racism in American law—the role of the law in promoting/alleviating racism)

http://stop-the-hate.org (Numerous links to anti-prejudice web sites)

http://www.pbs.org/newshour/bb/race_relations/race_relations.html (Stories from PBS's Online Newshour concerning issues of race)

KEY WORDS FOR PERIODICAL AND ONLINE SEARCHES
Prejudice
Race Discrimination
Race Relations
Racism

VIDEO PROGRAMS RELATED TO THIS TOPIC
Bridging Racial Divisions. Bureau for At-Risk Youth, 1997.
Cultures: Similarities and Differences. United Learning, 1997.
Pride and Prejudice: A History of Black Culture in America. Knowledge Unlimited, 1994.

ORGANIZATION TO CONTACT FOR ADDITIONAL INFORMATION
Center for Equal Opportunity, 815 Fifteenth Street, NW, Suite 928, Washington, DC 20005. Phone: 202–639–0803, Fax: 202–639–0827.

SUGGESTIONS FOR NARROWING THIS TOPIC
Debate the following question: Does affirmative action promote racism?

Discuss the reasons behind the failure of "bilingual education," which was introduced into federal legislation under Title VII of the Elementary and Secondary Education Act of 1968.

Research the history of integration into the U.S. military.

Research the treatment of Japanese Americans during World War II.

RELATED TOPICS
Apartheid
Civil Rights
Jewish Holocaust
Militia Groups

This RESEARCH TOPIC GUIDE is intended to help you find information on your topic in a wide variety of sources in this and any other library. Resources, though, are not limited to those described and not all libraries will have the same titles. Please ask a librarian for further guidance.

Runaways

BACKGROUND

A runaway is a child or teenager who has left home without parental permission. Approximately 1 million children or teens run away from home each year.

LOOK UNDER THE FOLLOWING SUBJECTS IN THE LIBRARY CATALOG

Runaway Children
Runaway Teenagers

BROWSE FOR BOOKS ON THE SHELF USING THIS CALL NUMBER

362.7 (Problems of Young People)

REFERENCE MATERIALS THAT MAY HELP (BOOKS OR CD-ROMS)

Arnest, Lauren Krohn. *Children, Young Adults, and the Law: A Dictionary.* ABC-CLIO, 1998.

Edmonds, Beverly C. and William R. Fernekes. *Children's Rights.* ABC-CLIO, 1996.

Exploring Law and Society. Gale Research, 1998. (CD-ROM)

Fremon, David K. *Running Away.* Marshall Cavendish, 1995.

Hempelman, Kathleen. *Teen Legal Rights: A Guide for the '90s.* Greenwood, 1994.

Stewart, Gail B. *Teen Runaways.* Lucent Books, 1997.

Wormser, Richard. *Juveniles in Trouble.* Julian Messner, 1994.

PERIODICAL INDEXES

EBSCO Magazine Article Summaries
InfoTrac
Reader's Guide to Periodical Literature
SIRS (Social Issues Resources Series)

SUGGESTED INTERNET SITES

http://www.covenanthouse.org (Home page of the largest privately funded childcare agency in the United States, providing shelter and service to homeless and runaway youths)

http://missingkids.org (Home page of the National Center for Missing and Exploited Children—includes education and resources, photos of missing children, success stories, and more)

http://www.vis.colostate.edu/~scriven/Runaway/resource.html (Suggested readings, national hotlines, and other organizations working on youth issues)

KEY WORDS FOR PERIODICAL AND ONLINE SEARCHES

Missing Persons
Runaway Children
Runaway Teenagers

VIDEO PROGRAMS RELATED TO THIS TOPIC

Getting Along with Parents. Live Wire, 1994.
Running Away, Dropping Out: Voices from Nightmare Street (Two-part series: Includes *Children of the Night* and *Starting Over*). Cambridge, 1994.
Teens and Tough Decisions. Pinnacle, 1989.

ORGANIZATIONS TO CONTACT FOR ADDITIONAL INFORMATION

National Center for Missing and Exploited Children, Suite 550, 2101 Wilson Boulevard, Arlington, VA 22201–3077. Phone: 703–235–3900, Fax: 703–235–4067.
Teen Rescue, PO Box 1463, Corona, CA 91719. Phone: 1–800–494–2200.

SUGGESTIONS FOR NARROWING THIS TOPIC

Create an educational poster or video illustrating how or where teenage runaways or teenagers in trouble can get help.
Create an educational poster or video aimed at parents outlining signs of a troubled teenager.
Discuss reasons that a teenager might run away from home.
Research laws regarding runaway children and teenagers.

RELATED TOPICS

Child Abduction
Dropouts
Homeless Persons

This RESEARCH TOPIC GUIDE is intended to help you find information on your topic in a wide variety of sources in this and any other library. Resources, though, are not limited to those described and not all libraries will have the same titles. Please ask a librarian for further guidance.

Shoplifting

BACKGROUND

Everyone in a society pays for the crimes of a few. This especially includes the crime of shoplifting. Approximately 10 percent of customers steal from stores. Stores ultimately must raise prices of their merchandise to compensate for theft and for detection systems.

LOOK UNDER THE FOLLOWING SUBJECTS IN THE LIBRARY CATALOG

Shoplifting

Stealing

BROWSE FOR BOOKS ON THE SHELF USING THIS CALL NUMBER

364.1 (Criminal Offenses)

REFERENCE MATERIALS THAT MAY HELP (BOOKS OR CD-ROMS)

Adams, Lisa K. *Dealing with Stealing*. Powerkids Press, 1998.

Durham, Jennifer L. *Crime in America*. ABC-CLIO, 1996.

Goldman, Marcus J. *Kleptomania: The Compulsion to Steal—What Can Be Done*. New Horizon Press, 1997.

Klemke, Lloyd W. *The Sociology of Shoplifting*. Praeger, 1992.

LeVert, Marianne. *Crime*. Facts on File, 1992.

Sennewald, Charles A. and John H. Christman. *Shoplifting*. Butterworth-Heinemann, 1992.

PERIODICAL INDEXES

EBSCO Magazine Article Summaries

InfoTrac

Reader's Guide to Periodical Literature

SIRS (Social Issues Resources Series)

SUGGESTED INTERNET SITES

http://www.halifax.cbc.ca/streetcents/crime/price.html (Questions and answers about costs of shoplifting)

http://www.wcei.com/familysafe/shoplift.htm (How shoplifting affects you and your family)

http://www.pixi.com/~521teen/214.htm (Is shoplifting stealing? An essay for teens)

KEY WORDS FOR PERIODICAL AND ONLINE SEARCHES

Shoplifting
Stealing
Theft

VIDEO PROGRAMS RELATED TO THIS TOPIC

Nobody Tells Me What To Do. Clearvue/eav, 1984.
Shoplifters: The Criminal Horde. Coronet, 1984.

SUGGESTIONS FOR NARROWING THIS TOPIC

Create an annotated chart illustrating the severity, costs to stores, and costs to
consumers of shoplifting.
Research laws and penalties regarding shoplifting.
Who shoplifts and why?

RELATED TOPICS

Addiction
Compulsive Behavior
Crime

This RESEARCH TOPIC GUIDE is intended to help you find information on your topic in a
wide variety of sources in this and any other library. Resources, though, are not limited to
those described and not all libraries will have the same titles. Please ask a librarian for further
guidance.

Tax Reform

BACKGROUND

In 1998, the Senate passed a bill that would eliminate the current tax code by December 31, 2002. What will replace it? The debate rages on!

LOOK UNDER THE FOLLOWING SUBJECTS IN THE LIBRARY CATALOG

Income Tax

Taxation

BROWSE FOR BOOKS ON THE SHELF USING THIS CALL NUMBER

336.2 (Taxes and Taxation)

REFERENCE MATERIALS THAT MAY HELP (BOOKS OR CD-ROMS)

Adams, Charles. *Those Dirty Rotten Taxes: The Tax Revolts that Built America*. Simon & Schuster, 1998.

Brownless, W. Eliot. *Federal Taxation in America: A Short History*. Cambridge University Press, 1996.

Graetz, Michael J. *The Decline (and Fall?) of the Income Tax*. W. W. Norton & Co., 1997.

Slemrod, Joel and Jon Bakija. *Taxing Ourselves: A Citizen's Guide to the Great Debate over Tax Reform*. MIT Press, 1998.

PERIODICAL INDEXES

EBSCO Magazine Article Summaries

InfoTrac

Reader's Guide to Periodical Literature

SIRS (Social Issues Resources Series)

SUGGESTED INTERNET SITES

http://flattax.house.gov (Site for Congressman Dick Armey's proposal to replace the current tax code with a flat, 17 percent rate)

http://www.ncpa.org/pi/taxes/tax7.html (Analysis of the flat tax)

http://www.washingtonpost.com/wp-srv/politics/special/security/security.htm (Overview, key stories, opinions, and related links regarding social security tax)

http://www.ssa.gov/history (Social Security history)

Http://www.taxation.org/ (Clearinghouse for various tax reform plans discussed by Congress, research and educational institutions, and politicians)

KEY WORD FOR PERIODICAL AND ONLINE SEARCHES

United States. Internal Revenue Service

VIDEO PROGRAM RELATED TO THIS TOPIC

Income Distribution and the Tax System. Films for the Humanities and Sciences, 1993.

ORGANIZATIONS TO CONTACT FOR ADDITIONAL INFORMATION

Americans for Tax Reform, 1320 10th Street, NW, Suite 200, Washington, DC 20036. Phone: 202–785–0266.

Heritage Foundation, 214 Massachusetts Avenue, NE, Washingon, DC 20002–4999. Phone: 202–546–4400, Fax: 202–546–8328.

SUGGESTIONS FOR NARROWING THIS TOPIC

Create an annotated timeline illustrating tax revolts and reforms throughout U.S. history.

Discuss the economic effects of the Taxation Act of 1986.

Discuss pros and cons of a flat tax.

Research the history of the Social Security tax.

RELATED TOPICS

Civil Disobedience

Welfare

This RESEARCH TOPIC GUIDE is intended to help you find information on your topic in a wide variety of sources in this and any other library. Resources, though, are not limited to those described and not all libraries will have the same titles. Please ask a librarian for further guidance.

Television Talk Shows

BACKGROUND

From Oprah to Sally to Jerry—television talk shows have a wide audience. Why are these shows so appealing? What motivates people to become guests on talk shows and reveal personal information?

LOOK UNDER THE FOLLOWING SUBJECTS IN THE LIBRARY CATALOG

Talk Shows

Television Programs

BROWSE FOR BOOKS ON THE SHELF USING THIS CALL NUMBER

741.45 (Television)

REFERENCE MATERIALS THAT MAY HELP (BOOKS OR CD-ROMS)

American Decades CD-ROM. Gale Research, 1997.

Calabro, Marian. *Zap: A Brief History of Television*. Four Winds Press, 1992.

Cohen, Eliot D. and Deni Elliott, eds. *Journalism Ethics*. ABC-CLIO, 1997.

Day, Nancy. *Sensational TV: Trash or Journalism?* Enslow, 1996.

Newton, David E. *Violence and the Media*. ABC-CLIO, 1996.

Owen, Rob. *Gen X TV: The Brady Bunch to Melrose Place*. Syracuse University Press, 1997.

PERIODICAL INDEXES

EBSCO Magazine Article Summaries

InfoTrac

Reader's Guide to Periodical Literature

SIRS (Social Studies Resources Series)

SUGGESTED INTERNET SITES

http://www.utexas.edu/coc/research/ntvs (University of Texas College of Communications National Television Violence Study)

http://www.urich.edu/~psych/tvortalk.html (Television morality and talk shows)

KEY WORDS FOR PERIODICAL AND ONLINE SEARCHES

Tabloid Television

Television Broadcasting—Talk Shows

VIDEO PROGRAMS RELATED TO THIS TOPIC

The Rise of the Television Talk Show. Films for the Humanities and Sciences, 1995.

Scott, Gini Graham. *Can We Talk: The Power and Influence of Talk Shows*. Insight Books, 1996.

Talked to Death: Have TV Talk Shows Gone Too Far? Films for the Humanities and Sciences, 1996.

Television and Human Behavior. Learning Seed, 1991.

ORGANIZATION TO CONTACT FOR ADDITIONAL INFORMATION

Parents Television Council, 600 Wilshire Boulevard, #700, Los Angeles, CA 90017. Phone: 213–629–9255.

SUGGESTIONS FOR NARROWING THIS TOPIC

Discuss how Oprah Winfrey has impacted reading in America.

Discuss the sensational nature of television talk shows.

Discuss positive aspects of television talk shows.

Research the evolution of the television talk show since the early 1970s.

RELATED TOPICS

Television Advertising

Television Children's Programming

Television News

This RESEARCH TOPIC GUIDE is intended to help you find information on your topic in a wide variety of sources in this and any other library. Resources, though, are not limited to those described and not all libraries will have the same titles. Please ask a librarian for further guidance.

Unmarried Teenage Fathers

BACKGROUND

Unmarried teenage fathers are twice as likely to drop out of school as single men without children. Economic and emotional issues surrounding teenage fatherhood can create havoc in both the lives of the father and of the child.

LOOK UNDER THE FOLLOWING SUBJECTS IN THE LIBRARY CATALOG

Teenage Fathers

Unmarried Fathers

BROWSE FOR BOOKS ON THE SHELF USING THESE CALL NUMBERS

305.23 (Young People)

306.85 (Unwed Parenthood)

362.7 (Problems of and Services to Young People)

REFERENCE MATERIALS THAT MAY HELP (BOOKS OR CD-ROMS)

Ayer, Eleanor H. *Everything You Need to Know about Teen Fatherhood.* Rosen, 1993.

Lang, Paul and Susan S. Lang. *Teen Fathers.* Franklin Watts, 1995.

Lindsay, Jeanne Warren. *Teen Dads: Rights, Responsibilities, and Joys.* Morning Glory, 1993.

Multimedia Teen Pregnancy. Clearvue/eav, 1996. (CD-ROM)

PERIODICAL INDEXES

EBSCO Magazine Article Summaries

InfoTrac

Reader's Guide to Periodical Literature

SIRS (Social Issues Resources Series)

SUGGESTED INTERNET SITES

http://www.kidscampaign.org/Whoseside/Maddads/myths-fathers.html
(Some myths about fatherlessness, and what can be done)

http://www.cis.yale.edu/ynhti/curriculum/guides/1994/1/94.01.03.x.html
(Minority teenage fathers, rights and responsibilities)

KEY WORDS FOR PERIODICAL AND ONLINE SEARCHES

Teenage Fathers

Unmarried Teenage Fathers

VIDEO PROGRAMS RELATED TO THIS TOPIC

Kids Having Kids: Teenage Pregnancy. Cambridge, 1992.

Kids Raising Kids: *Teenage Parenthood.* Cambridge, 1992.

Real People: Teen Mothers and Fathers Speak Out. Sunburst, 1995.

ORGANIZATION TO CONTACT FOR ADDITIONAL INFORMATION

National Center on Fathers and Families, c/o Vivian Gadsden, University of Pennsylvania, 3700 Walnut Street, Box 58, Philadelphia, PA 19104–6216. Phone: 215–573–5500.

SUGGESTIONS FOR NARROWING THIS TOPIC

Discuss the impact of fatherhood on a teenager.

How does a father's active presence affect a child's life?

Research legal issues regarding unmarried teenage fathers.

RELATED TOPICS

Ethics and Values

Teenage Mothers

This RESEARCH TOPIC GUIDE is intended to help you find information on your topic in a wide variety of sources in this and any other library. Resources, though, are not limited to those described and not all libraries will have the same titles. Please ask a librarian for further guidance.

V
Biography

Alexander the Great (356–323 B.C.)

BACKGROUND

Alexander II, known as Alexander the Great, lived from 356–323 B.C. Tutored by Aristotle in his youth, he became a great warrior and king over many lands including Greece and Persia.

LOOK UNDER THE FOLLOWING SUBJECT IN THE LIBRARY CATALOG

Alexander the Great

BROWSE FOR BOOKS ON THE SHELF USING THESE CALL NUMBERS

Biography section under Alexander the Great

938 (Greece to 323)

REFERENCE MATERIALS THAT MAY HELP (BOOKS OR CD-ROMS)

Ancient Greece and Rome. Charles Scribner's Sons, 1996.

Davis, Paul K. *Encyclopedia of Invasions and Conquests: From Ancient Times to the Present*. ABC-CLIO, 1996.

DISCovering Biography. Gale Research, 1997. (CD-ROM)

Encyclopedia of World Biography. Gale Research, 1998.

Nagel, Rob and Anne Commire. *World Leaders: People Who Shaped the World*. U.X.L., 1994.

PERIODICAL INDEXES

Biography Index

EBSCO Magazine Article Summaries

InfoTrac

Reader's Guide to Periodical Literature

SUGGESTED INTERNET SITES

http://www.goecities.com/Athens/Aegean/7545/Alexander.html (Biographical information on Alexander the Great and bibliography of resources)

http://www.pbs.org/mpt/alexander (In the Footsteps of Alexander the Great with Michael Wood—web site of the PBS special)

http://history.idbsu.edu/westciv/alexander/(History of Western Civilization course from Boise State University, Alexander the Great Unit)

KEY WORD FOR PERIODICAL AND ONLINE SEARCHES

Alexander the Great

VIDEO PROGRAMS RELATED TO THIS TOPIC

Alexander the Great. Clearvue/eav.

Alexander the Great: Battle of Issus. Ambrose, 1993.

In the Footsteps of Alexander the Great. PBS, 1998.

SUGGESTIONS FOR NARROWING THIS TOPIC

Create an annotated timeline illustrating the campaigns and battles of Alexander the Great.

Discuss the legacy of Alexander the Great.

Research the childhood of Alexander the Great.

RELATED TOPICS

Ancient Greece

Aristotle

Greek Mythology

This RESEARCH TOPIC GUIDE is intended to help you find information on your topic in a wide variety of sources in this and any other library. Resources, though, are not limited to those described and not all libraries will have the same titles. Please ask a librarian for further guidance.

Fidel Castro (1927–)

BACKGROUND

On New Year's Day, 1959, Fidel Castro and his forces made a victorious entry into Havana, having overrun the Batista government. The former lawyer became premier of Cuba in February of that year and his government began seizing U.S.-owned properties in Cuba. Castro allied himself and his government with communist countries.

LOOK UNDER THE FOLLOWING SUBJECTS IN THE LIBRARY CATALOG

Castro, Fidel

Cuba

Heads of States

BROWSE FOR BOOKS ON THE SHELF USING THESE CALL NUMBERS

Biography section under Castro, Fidel

920 (Collected Biography)

972.91 (Cuba)

REFERENCE MATERIALS THAT MAY HELP (BOOKS OR CD-ROMS)

DISCovering Biography. Gale Research, 1997. (CD-ROM)

Encyclopedia of World Biography. Gale Research, 1998.

Goldstone, Jack, ed. *The Encyclopedia of Political Revolutions*. Congressional Quarterly, 1998.

Leonard, Thomas M. *Castro and the Cuban Revolution*. Greenwood, 1999.

Tennebaum, Barbara A., ed. *Encyclopedia of Latin American History and Culture*. Charles Scribner's Sons, 1996.

U.X.L. Biographies. U.X.L., 1996. (CD-ROM)

PERIODICAL INDEXES

Biography Index

EBSCO Magazine Article Summaries

InfoTrac

Reader's Guide to Periodical Literature

SUGGESTED INTERNET SITES

http://www.lanic.utexas.edu/la/cb/cuba/castro.html (Search through the full-text English translations of Castro's speeches, interviews, and press conferences from 1959–1990) http://www.closeup.org/cuba.htm (U.S. policy toward Cuba—overview, timeline, links)

http://www.nocastro.com/ (Informs the public of atrocities and injustices of the Cuban government against its people)

http://www.cnn.com/resources/newsmakers/world/namerica/castro.html (CNN profile of Fidel Castro)

KEY WORDS FOR PERIODICAL AND ONLINE SEARCHES

Castro, Fidel

Cuba—Politics and Government

VIDEO PROGRAMS RELATED TO THIS TOPIC

Fidel Castro (*Biography* Series). A & E.

Portrait of Castro's Cuba. TBS, 1991.

SUGGESTIONS FOR NARROWING THIS TOPIC

Research the history of U.S.-Cuban relations since 1959.

Research life in Cuba under Castro's regime.

Research the overthrow of the Batista regime in 1959.

Write a biographical sketch of Fidel Castro.

RELATED TOPICS

Boat People

Communism

Cuban-Americans

This RESEARCH TOPIC GUIDE is intended to help you find information on your topic in a wide variety of sources in this and any other library. Resources, though, are not limited to those described and not all libraries will have the same titles. Please ask a librarian for further guidance.

Leonardo da Vinci (1452–1519)

BACKGROUND
Italian artist and scientist, Leonardo da Vinci was renowned for the breadth of his genius, which was exhibited by his astonishing quantity and quality of works and researches in a wide variety of disciplines.

LOOK UNDER THE FOLLOWING SUBJECT IN THE LIBRARY CATALOG
Leonardo da Vinci

BROWSE FOR BOOKS ON THE SHELF USING THESE CALL NUMBERS
Biography section under Leonardo da Vinci

920 (Collected Biography)

REFERENCE MATERIALS THAT MAY HELP (BOOKS OR CD-ROMS)
The Book of Art. Grolier, 1996.

DISCovering Biography. Gale Research, 1997. (CD-ROM)

Encyclopedia of World Biography. Gale Research, 1998.

Janson, H. W. and Anthony F. Janson. *History of Art for Young People*. Harry N. Abrams, 1987.

Leonardo da Vinci. Corbis, 1996. (CD-ROM)

Lomask, Milton. *Great Lives: Invention and Technology*. Charles Scribner's Sons, 1991.

U.X.L. Biographies. U.X.L., 1996. (CD-ROM)

PERIODICAL INDEXES
Biography Index

EBSCO Magazine Article Summaries

InfoTrac

Reader's Guide to Periodical Literature

SUGGESTED INTERNET SITES
http://library.advanced.org/3044 (Leonardo da Vinci: A Man of Both Worlds)

http://banzai.msi.umn.edu/leonardo (Drawings of Leonardo da Vinci)

KEY WORD FOR PERIODICAL AND ONLINE SEARCHES
Leonardo da Vinci

VIDEO PROGRAM RELATED TO THIS TOPIC

Leonardo da Vinci. Films for the Humanities and Sciences, 1989.

SUGGESTIONS FOR NARROWING THIS TOPIC

Discuss the importance to human scientific knowledge of Leonardo's sketchbook.

Discuss Leonardo's artistic style.

Discuss the "mystery" behind the painting of the *Mona Lisa de Gioconda*.

How was Leonardo a man ahead of his times?

RELATED TOPICS

Michaelangelo

Raphael

Renaissance

This RESEARCH TOPIC GUIDE is intended to help you find information on your topic in a wide variety of sources in this and any other library. Resources, though, are not limited to those described and not all libraries will have the same titles. Please ask a librarian for further guidance.

Diana, Princess of Wales (1961–1997)

BACKGROUND

Millions of people around the world mourned as they learned of the death of Diana, Princess of Wales, on August 31, 1997. Her style and charm, her devotion to her sons and her charities, had endeared her to an adoring public; and though she had divorced Prince Charles, she was still regarded by most as royalty.

LOOK UNDER THE FOLLOWING SUBJECT IN THE LIBRARY CATALOG

Diana, Princess of Wales

BROWSE FOR BOOKS ON THE SHELF USING THESE CALL NUMBERS

Biography section under Diana
920 (Collected Biography)

REFERENCE MATERIALS THAT MAY HELP (BOOKS OR CD-ROMS)

Current Biography. H. W. Wilson, date varies.
Diana, Princess of Wales CD-ROM. 1997. (Available from Library Video.)
DISCovering Biography. Gale Research, 1997. (CD-ROM)
Encyclopedia of World Biography. Gale Research, 1998.
U.X.L. Biographies. U.X.L., 1996. (CD-ROM)

PERIODICAL INDEXES

Biography Index
EBSCO Magazine Article Summaries
InfoTrac
Reader's Guide to Periodical Literature

SUGGESTED INTERNET SITES

http://cnn.com/WORLD/9708/diana/ (Multimedia history of Diana)
http://www.baronage.co.uk/bphtm-01/princess.html (Explanation of the title and the effect the royal divorce had on it)
http://ccwf.cc.utexas.edu/~cilldara/diana.html (A tribute to Diana and links to charities of which she was a patron)
http://www.royal.gov.uk/start.htm (The official royal Diana web site)

KEY WORD FOR PERIODICAL AND ONLINE SEARCHES

Diana, Princess of Wales

VIDEO PROGRAMS RELATED TO THIS TOPIC

Diana: A Celebration. BBC, 1997.

Princess Diana: In Search of Happiness. 1997. (Available from Library Video.)

ORGANIZATION TO CONTACT FOR ADDITIONAL INFORMATION

Diana, Princess of Wales Memorial Fund, Kensington Palace, London W8 4 PU, United Kingdom. Phone: 0171–9304832.

SUGGESTIONS FOR NARROWING THIS TOPIC

Discuss the media's attention to Diana and its effects on her.

Research Diana's childhood.

Research Diana's public role and charities.

RELATED TOPICS

British Royalty

Celebrity vs. Privacy

Divorce and Children

This RESEARCH TOPIC GUIDE is intended to help you find information on your topic in a wide variety of sources in this and any other library. Resources, though, are not limited to those described and not all libraries will have the same titles. Please ask a librarian for further guidance.

W.E.B. Du Bois (1868–1963)

BACKGROUND

One of the founders of the National Association for the Advancement of Colored People, William Edward Burghardt Du Bois was an educator, editor, and writer.

LOOK UNDER THE FOLLOWING SUBJECTS IN THE LIBRARY CATALOG

African American Authors
Du Bois, W.E.B.
National Association for the Advancement of Colored People

BROWSE FOR BOOKS ON THE SHELF USING THESE CALL NUMBERS

Biography section under Du Bois, W.E.B.
323 (Civil Rights)
920 (Collected Biography)

REFERENCE MATERIALS THAT MAY HELP (BOOKS OR CD-ROMS)

Contemporary Black Biography: Profiles from the International Black Community. Gale Research, date varies.
DISCovering Biography. Gale Research, 1997. (CD-ROM)
Encyclopedia of World Biography. Gale Research, 1998.
Franklin, John Hope and August Meier, eds. *Black Leaders of the Twentieth Century.* University of Illinois Press, 1982.
Metzger, Deborah A., et al., eds. *Black Writers.* Gale Research, 1988.
Straub, Deborah Gillan. *Contemporary Heroes and Heroines, Book II.* Gale Research, 1992.

PERIODICAL INDEXES

Biography Index
EBSCO Magazine Article Summaries
InfoTrac
Reader's Guide to Periodical Literature

SUGGESTED INTERNET SITES

http://www.duboislc.com/ (A good biography of W.E.B. Du Bois)
http://members.tripod.com/~DuBois/index.htm (Series of pages about life of Du Bois)

http://www.msu.edu/course/mc/112/1920s/Garvey-Dubois/index.html
(Voices which shaped our times—biographies, papers, and links about
Marcus Garvey and W.E.B. Du Bois)

http://www.unc.edu/~hsingerl/individs.html (American political thoughts:
Individual authors, including Du Bois)

KEY WORD FOR PERIODICAL AND ONLINE SEARCHES

Du Bois, W.E.B.

VIDEO PROGRAMS RELATED TO THIS TOPIC

W.E.B. Du Bois: Scholar and Activist. Schlessinger Video, 1994.

W.E.B. Du Bois of Great Barrington. PBS, 1997.

SUGGESTIONS FOR NARROWING THIS TOPIC

Discuss Du Bois's contributions to civil rights of African Americans.

Research Du Bois's political philosophy.

Research the controversy between Du Bois and Booker T. Washington.

Write a synopsis of one of Du Bois's major literary works.

RELATED TOPICS

Booker T. Washington

Civil Rights

This RESEARCH TOPIC GUIDE is intended to help you find information on your topic in a wide variety of sources in this and any other library. Resources, though, are not limited to those described and not all libraries will have the same titles. Please ask a librarian for further guidance.

Galileo Galilei (1564–1642)

BACKGROUND

Italian mathematician, astronomer, and physicist, Galileo (as he is commonly known) was first to use the telescope to study the skies. During his lifetime he made numerous scientific discoveries and was denounced by the Inquisition for some of his convictions.

LOOK UNDER THE FOLLOWING SUBJECT IN THE LIBRARY CATALOG

Galilei, Galileo

BROWSE FOR BOOKS ON THE SHELF USING THESE CALL NUMBERS

Biography section under Galilei, Galileo
920 (Collected Biography)

REFERENCE MATERIALS THAT MAY HELP (BOOKS OR CD-ROMS)

Biographical Encyclopedia of Scientists. Marshall Cavendish, 1998.
Dictionary of Scientific Biography. Charles Scribner's Sons, 1970–1990.
DISCovering Biography. Gale Research, 1997. (CD-ROM)
Encyclopedia of World Biography. Gale Research, 1998.
Scientists. U.X.L., 1996.
U.X.L. Science CD. U.X.L., 1997. (CD-ROM)

PERIODICAL INDEXES

Biography Index
EBSCO Magazine Article Summaries
InfoTrac
Reader's Guide to Periodical Literature
TOM Health and Science

SUGGESTED INTERNET SITES

http://es.rice.edu/ES/humsoc/Galileo/ (The Galileo Project from Rice University—a hypertext source of information on the life and works of Galileo Galilei and the science of his time)
http://webug.physics.uiuc.edu/courses/phys150/fall97/slides/lect06/ (Galileo: Astronomy and physics, with information on his contributions in both areas)

http://galileo.imss.firenze.it/museo/b/egalilg.html (Biographical information on Galileo from the Institute and Museum of the History of Science of Florence, Italy)

http://www.knight.org/advent/cathen/06342b.htm (From the Catholic Encyclopedia, the history of Galileo's scientific conflict with the Catholic Church)

KEY WORD FOR PERIODICAL AND ONLINE SEARCHES

Galileo

VIDEO PROGRAMS RELATED TO THIS TOPIC

Galileo: The Challenge of Reason. Learning Corporation of America, 1974.
Galileo Galilei Moves the Earth. Hawkhill Associates, 1994.

SUGGESTIONS FOR NARROWING THIS TOPIC

Create an annotated timeline illustrating Galileo's discoveries and accomplishments.

Discuss the denouncement of Galileo by the Catholic Church and the Inquisition.

Research Galileo's contributions in mechanics.

Research Galileo's work with the telescope and his observations of the sky.

RELATED TOPICS

Johannes Kepler
Nicholas Copernicus
Solar System

This RESEARCH TOPIC GUIDE is intended to help you find information on your topic in a wide variety of sources in this and any other library. Resources, though, are not limited to those described and not all libraries will have the same titles. Please ask a librarian for further guidance.

Mohandas (Mahatma) Karamchand Gandhi (1869-1948)

BACKGROUND

Spiritual leader of India and considered the father of his country, Mahatma Gandhi led campaigns of civil disobedience in Natal and in India against the unfair British-led governments.

LOOK UNDER THE FOLLOWING SUBJECT IN THE LIBRARY CATALOG

Gandhi, Mohandas

BROWSE FOR BOOKS ON THE SHELF USING THESE CALL NUMBERS

Biography section under Gandhi, Mohandas

920 (Collected Biography)

REFERENCE MATERIALS THAT MAY HELP (BOOKS OR CD-ROMS)

Brown, Ray B., et al., eds. *Contemporary Heroes and Heroines*. Gale Research, 1990.

DISCovering Biography. Gale Research, 1997. (CD-ROM)

Encyclopedia of World Biography. Gale Research, 1998.

Jacobs, William Jay. *Great Lives: World Government*. Charles Scribner's Sons, 1992.

Nagel, Rob and Anne Commire. *World Leaders: People Who Shaped the World*. U.X.L., 1994.

Wuthnow, Robert, ed. *Encyclopedia of Politics and Religion*. Princeton University Press, 1998.

PERIODICAL INDEXES

Biography Index

EBSCO Magazine Article Summaries

InfoTrac

Reader's Guide to Periodical Literature

SUGGESTED INTERNET SITES

http://www.cbu.edu/Gandhi (Home page of the M. K. Gandhi Institute for Nonviolence)

http://www.engagedpage.com/gandhi.html (Brief history and works of Gandhi) http://norfacad.pvt.k12.va.us/project/gandhi/gandhi.htm (Biography of Gandhi and links to other related sites)

KEY WORDS FOR PERIODICAL AND ONLINE SEARCHES

Gandhi, Mahatma
Gandhi, Mohandas

VIDEO PROGRAMS RELATED TO THIS TOPIC

Gandhi. Granada Video, 1989.
Gandhi. Columbia, 1990.
Gandhi: Pilgrim of Peace. A & E, 1994.

ORGANIZATION TO CONTACT FOR ADDITIONAL INFORMATION

M. K. Gandhi Institute for Nonviolence, Christian Brothers University, 650 East Parkway South, Memphis, TN 38104. Phone: 901–452–2824, Fax: 901–452–2775.

SUGGESTIONS FOR NARROWING THIS TOPIC

Discuss Gandhi's nonviolent protests against the British government.
Discuss Gandhi's influence in nonviolent movements around the world.
Explain Gandhi's "Eight Blunders of the World."
Research Gandhi's early life and education.

RELATED TOPICS

Civil Disobedience
Hinduism
India
Martin Luther King, Jr.

This RESEARCH TOPIC GUIDE is intended to help you find information on your topic in a wide variety of sources in this and any other library. Resources, though, are not limited to those described and not all libraries will have the same titles. Please ask a librarian for further guidance.

Adolf Hitler (1889–1945)

BACKGROUND

Adolf Hitler was dictator of Germany from 1933 to 1945. Under his government, the Third Reich, and with his Nazi political party and his secret police, the Gestapo, Hitler embarked on a campaign of hatred that resulted in the enslavement and murder of millions of Jews from all over Europe.

LOOK UNDER THE FOLLOWING SUBJECTS IN THE LIBRARY CATALOG

> Germany—History
> Hitler, Adolf
> Jewish Holocaust (1933–1945)
> National Socialism

BROWSE FOR BOOKS ON THE SHELF USING THESE CALL NUMBERS

> Biography section under Hitler, Adolf
> 320.5 (Political Ideologies, including National Socialism)
> 940.53 (Jewish Holocaust)
> 943.086 (Germany during the Third Reich, 1933–1945)

REFERENCE MATERIALS THAT MAY HELP (BOOKS OR CD-ROMS)

> *DISCovering Biography*. Gale Research, 1997. (CD-ROM)
> *Encyclopedia of World Biography*. Gale Research, 1998.
> *Fascist Dictatorships*. Clearvue/eav, 1994. (CD-ROM)
> Jacobs, William Jay. *Great Lives: World Government*. Charles Scribner's Sons, 1992.
> Nagel, Rob and Anne Commire. *World Leaders: People Who Shaped the World*. U.X.L., 1994.

PERIODICAL INDEXES

> *Biography Index*
> *EBSCO Magazine Article Summaries*
> *InfoTrac*
> *Reader's Guide to Periodical Literature*

SUGGESTED INTERNET SITES

> http://www.crusader.net/texts/mk/index.html (Text of *Mein Kampf* by Adolf Hitler)

http://www.historyplace.com/worldwar2/riseofhitler/index.htm (*The Rise of Hitler* from *The History Place*)

http://www.cfcsc.dnd.ca/links/bio/hitler.html (Military and diplomatic biography of Adolf Hitler)

http://remember.org/guide/index.html#Facts (An instructional guide for teachers on the Holocaust; includes biographical information on Adolf Hitler)

KEY WORDS FOR PERIODICAL AND ONLINE SEARCHES

Hitler, Adolf
Jewish Holocaust
Nazism
World War II

VIDEO PROGRAMS RELATED TO THIS TOPIC

Heil Hitler! Confessions of a Hitler Youth. HBO, 1991.
Hitler: The Final Chapter. Central Park, 1995.
The Life of Adolf Hitler. Video Yesteryear, 1961.
Schindler's List. MCA Home Video, 1993.

SUGGESTIONS FOR NARROWING THIS TOPIC

Discuss Hitler's role in World War I and the effect it had upon him.
Research the Beer Hall Putsch and Hitler's subsequent trial for treason.
Research Hitler's rise to power.
Why did millions of German youth become as loyal to Hitler as to a father?

RELATED TOPICS

Anti-semitism
Jewish Holocaust
Nazism
World War II

This RESEARCH TOPIC GUIDE is intended to help you find information on your topic in a wide variety of sources in this and any other library. Resources, though, are not limited to those described and not all libraries will have the same titles. Please ask a librarian for further guidance.

Joan of Arc (1412–1431)

BACKGROUND

French national heroine and patron saint, Joan of Arc was born a peasant. At the age of thirteen, she began hearing voices urging her to save France and its king, Charles VII. She led the French army against the English during the Hundred Years War, was subsequently captured, sold to the English, and burned at the stake in Rouen.

LOOK UNDER THE FOLLOWING SUBJECT IN THE LIBRARY CATALOG

Jeanne d'Arc

BROWSE FOR BOOKS ON THE SHELF USING THIS CALL NUMBER

Biography section under Jeanne d'Arc

REFERENCE MATERIALS THAT MAY HELP (BOOKS OR CD-ROMS)

DISCovering Biography. Gale Research, 1997. (CD-ROM)
Encyclopedia of World Biography. Gale Research, 1998.
Nagel, Rob and Anne Commire. *World Leaders: People Who Shaped the World*. U.X.L., 1994.
U.X.L. Biographies. U.X.L., 1996. (CD-ROM)

PERIODICAL INDEXES

Biography Index
EBSCO Magazine Article Summaries
Index to *History Today* Magazine
InfoTrac
Reader's Guide to Periodical Literature

SUGGESTED INTERNET SITES

http://www.gale.com/gale/cwh/joan.html (Biography of Joan of Arc from Celebrating Women's History)
http://www.labs.net/dmccormick/jeanne.htm (Examination of the theory that Joan of Arc was a member of an ancient pagan cult, and her death was a ritual sacrifice)
http://www.catholic.org/saints/saints/joanarc.html (Catholic Online Saints: St. Joan of Arc)

KEY WORDS FOR PERIODICAL AND ONLINE SEARCHES

Joan of Arc
Joan, of Arc, Saint
St. Joan of Arc

VIDEO PROGRAM RELATED TO THIS TOPIC

Joan of Arc. A & E, 1998.

SUGGESTIONS FOR NARROWING THIS TOPIC

Discuss the canonization of Joan of Arc.
How did Joan of Arc, a young girl, convince the King of France and his tribunal to assign an army to her to lead in a military campaign?
Research Joan of Arc's imprisonment and trials.
What evidences are there that Joan of Arc was truly guided by divine voices?

RELATED TOPICS

Charlemagne
Hundred Years War
Middle Ages
Thomas á Becket

This RESEARCH TOPIC GUIDE is intended to help you find information on your topic in a wide variety of sources in this and any other library. Resources, though, are not limited to those described and not all libraries will have the same titles. Please ask a librarian for further guidance.

Martin Luther King, Jr. (1929–1968)

BACKGROUND

Ordained minister and civil rights leader, Martin Luther King, Jr. was an advocate of nonviolence. He was awarded the Nobel Peace Prize in 1964 for his efforts to bring about peaceful desegregation in the South.

LOOK UNDER THE FOLLOWING SUBJECTS IN THE LIBRARY CATALOG

African Americans—Biography

Civil Rights

King, Martin Luther, Jr.

BROWSE FOR BOOKS ON THE SHELF USING THESE CALL NUMBERS

Biography section under King, Martin Luther, Jr.

323 (Civil Rights)

920 (Collected Biography)

REFERENCE MATERIALS THAT MAY HELP (BOOKS OR CD-ROMS)

Conyers, James L., ed. *Black Lives: Essays in African American Biography.* M. E. Sharpe, 1998.

DISCovering Biography. Gale Research, 1997. (CD-ROM)

Encyclopedia of World Biography. Gale Research, 1998.

Franklin, John Hope and August Meier. *Black Leaders of the Twentieth Century.* University of Illinois Press, 1982.

Lowery, Charles D. and John F. Marszalek, eds. *Encyclopedia of African-American Civil Rights: From Emancipation to the Present.* Greenwood, 1992.

Nagel, Rob and Anne Commire. *World Leaders: People Who Shaped the World.* U.X.L., 1994.

PERIODICAL INDEXES

Biography Index

EBSCO Magazine Article Summaries

InfoTrac

Reader's Guide to Periodical Literature

SUGGESTED INTERNET SITES

http://home.stlnet.com/~cdstelzer/mlk.html (Questions regarding the murder of Martin Luther King, Jr.)

http://www.stanford.edu/group/King/ (Primary and secondary documents about Martin Luther King, Jr.)

http://www.seattletimes.com/mlk (A tribute to Martin Luther King, Jr. from the *Seattle Times*)

KEY WORD FOR PERIODICAL AND ONLINE SEARCHES

King, Martin Luther, Jr.

VIDEO PROGRAMS RELATED TO THIS TOPIC

At the River I Stand. Memphis State University, 1993.

Dr. Martin Luther King, Jr.: A Historical Perspective. Xenon, 1993.

Martin Luther King, Jr. Library Video, 1992.

Martin Luther King, Jr.—The Man and the Dream: Biography. BBC/A & E, 1997.

ORGANIZATION TO CONTACT FOR ADDITIONAL INFORMATION

The Martin Luther King, Jr. Center for Nonviolent Social Change, 449 Auburn Avenue, N.E., Atlanta, GA 30312. Phone: 404–524–1956.

SUGGESTIONS FOR NARROWING THIS TOPIC

Create an annotated timeline illustrating major events in King's life.

Discuss the controversy surrounding King's murder.

Discuss: Is Martin Luther King, Jr.'s "dream" still alive?

What made Martin Luther King, Jr. a great leader?

RELATED TOPICS

Brown v. Board of Education (Supreme Court Case)

Malcolm X

Medgar Evers

Mohandas Gandhi

This RESEARCH TOPIC GUIDE is intended to help you find information on your topic in a wide variety of sources in this and any other library. Resources, though, are not limited to those described and not all libraries will have the same titles. Please ask a librarian for further guidance.

Isaac Newton (1642–1721)

BACKGROUND

English physicist and mathematician, Isaac Newton is perhaps best known popularly for having conceived the idea of universal gravitation after seeing an apple fall in his garden; but his body of work was astounding in both quantity and quality, and his influence in both science and mathematics remains of enduring significance.

LOOK UNDER THE FOLLOWING SUBJECTS IN THE LIBRARY CATALOG

Mathematicians
Newton, Isaac
Scientists

BROWSE FOR BOOKS ON THE SHELF USING THESE CALL NUMBERS

Biography section under Newton, Isaac
509.2 (Scientists)
510.92 (Mathematicians)
920 (Collected Biography)

REFERENCE MATERIALS THAT MAY HELP (BOOKS OR CD-ROMS)

Biographical Encyclopedia of Mathematicians. Marshall Cavendish, 1999.
Dictionary of Scientific Biography. Macmillan Library Reference, 1998.
DISCovering Biography. Gale Research, 1997. (CD-ROM)
Encyclopedia of World Biography. Gale Research, 1998.
Macmillan Encyclopedia of Science. Macmillan Reference, 1997.

PERIODICAL INDEXES

Biography Index
EBSCO Magazine Article Summaries
InfoTrac
Reader's Guide to Periodical Literature
TOM Health and Science

SUGGESTED INTERNET SITES

Http://www.maths.tcd.ie/pub/HistMath/People/Newton/RouseBall/
RB_Newton.html (Biography of Newton, taken from *A Short Account of the History of Mathematics*, 4th ed., 1908, by W. W. Rouse Ball)

http://www.fordham.edu/halsall/mod/newton-princ.html (Excerpts of Newton's text on *The Mathematical Principles of Natural Philosophy)*
http://www.newton.cam.ac.uk/newtlife.html (Newton's life)
http://www.astro.virginia.edu/~eww6n/bios/Newton.html (Biographical
sketch of Newton, including hypertext links)

KEY WORD FOR PERIODICAL AND ONLINE SEARCHES

Newton, Isaac

VIDEO PROGRAM RELATED TO THIS TOPIC

Newton: The Mind that Found the Future. Learning Corporation of America.

SUGGESTIONS FOR NARROWING THIS TOPIC

Create an annotated timeline summarizing Newton's contributions to science
and mathematics.
Discuss the priority dispute involving Newton's invention of calculus.
Explain the scientific method invented by Newton and its significance.
What influence did Halley have upon Newton's scientific work?

RELATED TOPICS

Age of Reason
Aristotle
Galileo
John Philoponus

This RESEARCH TOPIC GUIDE is intended to help you find information on your topic in a
wide variety of sources in this and any other library. Resources, though, are not limited to
those described and not all libraries will have the same titles. Please ask a librarian for further
guidance.

Louis Pasteur (1822–1895)

BACKGROUND

Louis Pasteur, French scientist, is perhaps most famous for his development of pasteurization and for the development of a vaccine for rabies.

LOOK UNDER THE FOLLOWING SUBJECT IN THE LIBRARY CATALOG

Pasteur, Louis

BROWSE FOR BOOKS ON THE SHELF USING THESE CALL NUMBERS

Biography section under Pasteur, Louis
920 (Collected Biography)

REFERENCE MATERIALS THAT MAY HELP (BOOKS OR CD-ROMS)

Curtis, Robert H. *Great Lives: Medicine*. Charles Scribner's Sons, 1993.
Dictionary of Scientific Biography. Macmillan Library Reference, 1998.
DISCovering Biography. Gale Research, 1997. (CD-ROM)
Encyclopedia of World Biography. Gale Research, 1998.

PERIODICAL INDEXES

Biography Index
EBSCO Magazine Article Summaries
InfoTrac
Reader's Guide to Periodical Literature
TOM Health and Science

SUGGESTED INTERNET SITES

http://www.pasteur.fr/Pasteur/presentation-uk.html (Louis Pasteur and the Pasteur Institute)
http://www.ambafrance.org/HYPERLAB/PEOPLE/_pasteur.html (His life and works)

KEY WORD FOR PERIODICAL AND ONLINE SEARCHES

Pasteur, Louis

VIDEO PROGRAM RELATED TO THIS TOPIC

Louis Pasteur Proves Germs Cause Disease. Hawkhill, 1994.

SUGGESTIONS FOR NARROWING THIS TOPIC

Discuss AIDS research at the Pasteur Institute.

Create an annotated timeline summarizing Pasteur's discoveries.

Describe Pasteur's scientific theory and methodology.

Discuss how Pasteur's discoveries have improved the human condition.

RELATED TOPICS

Edward Jenner

Jonas Salk

Joseph Lister

Microscope

This RESEARCH TOPIC GUIDE is intended to help you find information on your topic in a wide variety of sources in this and any other library. Resources, though, are not limited to those described and not all libraries will have the same titles. Please ask a librarian for further guidance.

Elvis Aaron Presley (1935–1977)

BACKGROUND

Referred to as "The King of Rock and Roll," Elvis Presley worked as a truck driver in Memphis before becoming a music legend. He starred in 33 films and sold over a billion records.

LOOK UNDER THE FOLLOWING SUBJECTS IN THE LIBRARY CATALOG

Musicians

Presley, Elvis

BROWSE FOR BOOKS ON THE SHELF USING THESE CALL NUMBERS

Biography section under Presley, Elvis

780.92 (Musicians)

920 (Collected Biography)

REFERENCE MATERIALS THAT MAY HELP (BOOKS OR CD-ROMS)

DISCovering Biography. Gale Research, 1997. (CD-ROM)

Encyclopedia of World Biography. Gale Research, 1998.

Knapp, Ron. *American Legends of Rock*. Enslow, 1996.

LaBlanc, Michael L., ed. *Contemporary Musicians: Profiles of the People in Music*. Gale Research, 1989.

Severson, Molly, ed. *Performing Artists*. U.X.L., 1995.

U.X.L. Biographies. U.X.L., 1996. (CD-ROM)

PERIODICAL INDEXES

Biography Index

EBSCO Magazine Article Summaries

InfoTrac

Reader's Guide to Periodical Literature

SUGGESTED INTERNET SITES

http://sunsite.unc.edu/elvis/elvishom.html (The original "unofficial" Elvis home page)

http://www.elvis-presley.com/ (The Official Worldwide Website of Elvis Presley's Graceland)

http://users.aol.com/petedixon/elvis/index.html (The Complete Elvis database) http://www.chron.com/content/houston/interactive/voyager/elvis/features/txmag.html (Eternally Elvis—article from the *Houston Chronicle*)

KEY WORD FOR PERIODICAL AND ONLINE SEARCHES

Presley, Elvis

VIDEO PROGRAMS RELATED TO THIS TOPIC

Elvis on Tour. MGM/UA Video, 1997.
Elvis Presley: The Complete Story. Passport International, 1998.
Love Me Tender. CBS/Fox Home Video, 1986.
This Is Elvis. Warner Home Video, 1986.

ORGANIZATION TO CONTACT FOR ADDITIONAL INFORMATION

Graceland, PO Box 16508, Memphis, TN 38186–0508. Phone: 901–332–3322, 1–800–238–2000.

SUGGESTIONS FOR NARROWING THIS TOPIC

Discuss Elvis's drug use.
Discuss Elvis's relationship with his mother.
Research the controversy surrounding Elvis's death.
Research Elvis's childhood and rise to fame.
Why will Elvis Presley's legend not die?

RELATED TOPICS

The Beatles
Popular Culture of the 50s and 60s
Rock and Roll Music

This RESEARCH TOPIC GUIDE is intended to help you find information on your topic in a wide variety of sources in this and any other library. Resources, though, are not limited to those described and not all libraries will have the same titles. Please ask a librarian for further guidance.

Mother Teresa (1910–1997)

BACKGROUND

Mother Teresa of Calcutta was born Agnes Gonxha Bojaxhiu in Albania to Catholic, middle-class parents. She made the decision to become a nun at the age of 18 and chose the name Sister Teresa in memory of the Little Teresa of Lisieux.

LOOK UNDER THE FOLLOWING SUBJECT IN THE LIBRARY CATALOG

Teresa, Mother

BROWSE FOR BOOKS ON THE SHELF USING THESE CALL NUMBERS

Biography section under Teresa, Mother
920 (Collected Biography)

REFERENCE MATERIALS THAT MAY HELP (BOOKS OR CD-ROMS)

Current Biography. H. W. Wilson, date varies.
DISCovering Biography. Gale Research, 1997. (CD-ROM)
Encyclopedia of World Biography. Gale Research, 1998.
U.X.L. Biographies. U.X.L., 1996. (CD-ROM)
Vernoff, Edward and Rima Shore. *The International Dictionary of 20th Century Biography.* New American Library, 1987.

PERIODICAL INDEXES

Biography Index
EBSCO Magazine Article Summaries
InfoTrac
Reader's Guide to Periodical Literature

SUGGESTED INTERNET SITES

http://www.almaz.com/nobel/peace/1979a.html (The Nobel Prize Internet Archive—information and links about Mother Teresa)
http://www.S2F.com/stanmeyer/ann/stories/aweb2.html (Helping the helpless—Mother Teresa and her Missionaries of Charity)
http://www.tisv.be/mt/indmt.htm (Mother Teresa: life, works, links)

KEY WORDS FOR PERIODICAL AND ONLINE SEARCHES

Missionaries of Charity

Teresa, Mother

VIDEO PROGRAM RELATED TO THIS TOPIC

Mother Teresa: In the Name of God's Poor. Hallmark, 1997.

ORGANIZATION TO CONTACT FOR ADDITIONAL INFORMATION

Missionaries of Charity, 54A Acharya Jagadish Chandra Bose Road, Calcutta, WB 700016, India. Phone: 091–033–245–2277.

SUGGESTIONS FOR NARROWING THIS TOPIC

Create an annotated timeline outlining the life and works of Mother Teresa.

Discuss the commonalities between Mother Teresa and the eight other women who have won the Nobel Peace Prize.

Research Mother Teresa's childhood.

Research the origins and works of the Missionaries of Charity.

RELATED TOPICS

India

Mohandas Gandhi

Poverty

This RESEARCH TOPIC GUIDE is intended to help you find information on your topic in a wide variety of sources in this and any other library. Resources, though, are not limited to those described and not all libraries will have the same titles. Please ask a librarian for further guidance.

United States Members of Congress

BACKGROUND

The systematic search as outlined below can be used to research any member of the U.S. Congress.

LOOK UNDER THE FOLLOWING SUBJECTS IN THE LIBRARY CATALOG

Search under the name of the Congress member, last name first.
United States. Congress

BROWSE FOR BOOKS ON THE SHELF USING THESE CALL NUMBERS

Biography section under the last name of the Congress member
328.73 (Congress)
920 (Collected Biography)

REFERENCE MATERIALS THAT MAY HELP (BOOKS OR CD-ROMS)

Congressional Staff Directory. Congressional Quarterly, date varies.
Congressional Yearbook. Congressional Quarterly, date varies.
Current Biography Yearbook. H. W. Wilson, date varies.
Kaptur, Marcy. *Women of Congress: A Twentieth-Century Odyssey*. Congressional Quarterly, 1996.
Sharpe, Michael. *Directory of Congressional Voting Scores and Interest Group Ratings*. Congressional Quarterly, 1997.

PERIODICAL INDEXES

Biography Index
EBSCO Magazine Article Summaries
InfoTrac
Reader's Guide to Periodical Literature
SIRS (Social Issues Resources Series)

SUGGESTED INTERNET SITES

http://www.geocities.com/CapitolHill/1411/index.html (E-mail addresses for the U.S. Congress)
http://www.capweb.net/ (The Internet Guide to the U.S. Congress)
http://www.rollcall.com/ (Twice-weekly news and commentary from the heart of Capitol Hill)

KEY WORDS FOR PERIODICAL AND ONLINE SEARCHES

Search under the last name of the Congress member.

United States. Congress

VIDEO PROGRAMS RELATED TO THIS TOPIC

Congress: What It Is, How It Works and How It Affects You. Guidance Associates, 1990.

A Day in the Life of Congress. American School Publishers, 1992.

ORGANIZATIONS TO CONTACT FOR ADDITIONAL INFORMATION

To contact a member of the U.S. Senate send a letter to: Office of Senator___, U.S. Senate, Washington, DC 20510.

SUGGESTIONS FOR NARROWING THIS TOPIC

Discuss major accomplishments of a selected member of Congress.

Discuss the political beliefs/agenda of a selected member of Congress.

Research recent legislation introduced by a selected member of Congress.

Write a biographical essay of a selected member of Congress.

RELATED TOPICS

The U.S. Presidency

The U.S. Supreme Court

This RESEARCH TOPIC GUIDE is intended to help you find information on your topic in a wide variety of sources in this and any other library. Resources, though, are not limited to those described and not all libraries will have the same titles. Please ask a librarian for further guidance.

United States Presidents

BACKGROUND

Research on any U.S. president of your choice can proceed in the following orderly procedure.

LOOK UNDER THE FOLLOWING SUBJECTS IN THE LIBRARY CATALOG

> Presidents, United States
> Search under the name of the president, last name first.

BROWSE FOR BOOKS ON THE SHELF USING THESE CALL NUMBERS

> Biography section under the last name of the president
> 353.03 (Administration of the President of U.S.)
> 920 (Collected Biography)

REFERENCE MATERIALS THAT MAY HELP (BOOKS OR CD-ROMS)

> *DISCovering Biography*. Gale Research, 1997. (CD-ROM)
> *DISCovering U.S. History*. Gale Research, 1997. (CD-ROM)
> Kane, Joseph Nathan. *Facts about the Presidents*. H. W. Wilson, 1989.
> Rubel, David. *Encyclopedia of the Presidents and their Times*. Scholastic Reference, 1994.
> Whitney, David C. and Robin Vaughn Whitney. *The American Presidents*. Reader's Digest Association, 1996.
> *World Book of America's Presidents: Portraits of the Presidents*. World Book, 1995.

PERIODICAL INDEXES

> *Biography Index*
> *EBSCO Magazine Article Summaries*
> Index to *American Heritage* Magazine
> *InfoTrac*
> *Reader's Guide to Periodical Literature*

SUGGESTED INTERNET SITES

> http://www.gl.umbc.edu/~cgehrm1/gpoaframes.html (The Great Presidential Outline Archive: Outlines of most of the presidents from 1780–Present)
> http://www.pbs.org/wgbh/pages/amex/presidents/indexjs.html (From PBS series, *The American Experience*, extensive site on the Presidents of the United States)

http://www.grolier.com/presidents/preshome.html (The American Presidency, a site from Grolier Online, which presents history of presidents, the presidency, politics, and related subjects)

http://www.ipl.org/ref/POTUS (The Internet Public Library: Presidents of the United States—background information, election results, cabinet members, notable events, points of interest, and links for each president)

http://www.columbia.edu/acis/bartleby/inaugural (Inaugural addresses of the presidents)

KEY WORDS FOR PERIODICAL AND ONLINE SEARCHES

Presidents, U.S.

Search under the name of the president you are researching.

VIDEO PROGRAMS RELATED TO THIS TOPIC

Portraits of American Presidents (3 videos). NBC News/Questar, 1992.

The Presidency. Rainbow, 1993.

The President and the Presidency. Knowledge Unlimited, 1998.

Presidents/First Ladies. ABC News, 1990.

SUGGESTIONS FOR NARROWING THIS TOPIC

Create an annotated timeline depicting events of a selected president's administration.

Discuss the domestic policy of a selected president.

Research controversies surrounding a selected president.

Research major accomplishments of a selected president.

Write a biographical essay of a selected president.

RELATED TOPICS

Constitution

First Ladies

Political Parties

Political Systems

This RESEARCH TOPIC GUIDE is intended to help you find information on your topic in a wide variety of sources in this and any other library. Resources, though, are not limited to those described and not all libraries will have the same titles. Please ask a librarian for further guidance.

Queen Victoria (1819-1901)

BACKGROUND

Queen Victoria, the longest reigning British monarch and Empress of India, assumed the throne at age 18. She married Albert, Prince of Saxe-Coburg-Gotha, and bore nine children. During her reign, Great Britain became the most powerful nation in the world.

LOOK UNDER THE FOLLOWING SUBJECTS IN THE LIBRARY CATALOG

Kings, Queens, Rulers, etcetera
Victoria, Queen of Great Britain

BROWSE FOR BOOKS ON THE SHELF USING THESE CALL NUMBERS

Biography section under Victoria
920 (Collected Biography)

REFERENCE MATERIALS THAT MAY HELP (BOOKS OR CD-ROMS)

DISCovering Biography. Gale Research, 1997. (CD-ROM)
Encyclopedia of World Biography. Gale Research, 1998.
Jackson, Guida M. *Women Who Ruled*. ABC-CLIO, 1990.
Jacobs, William Jay. *Great Lives: World Government*. Charles Scribner's
    Sons, 1992.

PERIODICAL INDEXES

Biography Index
EBSCO Magazine Article Summaries
InfoTrac
Reader's Guide to Periodical Literature

SUGGESTED INTERNET SITES

http://www.engl.Virginia.edu/~mhc/Victoria.html (Numerous images of
    Queen Victoria)
http://www.camelotintl.com/heritage/victoria.html (British and Irish Heritage: Biography of Queen Victoria)
http://www.indiana.edu/~victoria/ (The Victoria Research Web)
http://www.victoriana.com/doors/queenvictoria.htm (Queen Victoria's not
    so "Victorian" writings about pregnancy, children, marriage, and men)

KEY WORDS FOR PERIODICAL AND ONLINE SEARCHES

Queen Victoria
Victoria, Queen of Great Britain

VIDEO PROGRAMS RELATED TO THIS TOPIC

Queen Victoria and British History: 1837–1901. Coronet, 1977.
The Victorian Age. Guidance Associates.

SUGGESTIONS FOR NARROWING THIS TOPIC

Create an annotated timeline which highlights major events and advancements during Victoria's reign.

Create a family tree which illustrates why Victoria is described as the "Grandmother of Europe."

Discuss Prince Albert's influence upon Victoria and the monarchy.

How did Victoria become an influence upon the "Victorian" mentality?

RELATED TOPICS

Charles Dickens
Irish Potato Famine
Prince Albert
Victorian Society

This RESEARCH TOPIC GUIDE is intended to help you find information on your topic in a wide variety of sources in this and any other library. Resources, though, are not limited to those described and not all libraries will have the same titles. Please ask a librarian for further guidance.

Alice Walker (1944-   )

BACKGROUND

Pulitzer Prize winner novelist and poet, Alice Walker began her life in Eatonton, Georgia, the eighth child of poor sharecroppers. She graduated high school as valedictorian of her class and attended Spellman College in Atlanta, where she became involved in the Civil Rights Movement. Her novel, *The Color Purple*, published in 1982, became a motion picture directed by Steven Spielberg.

LOOK UNDER THE FOLLOWING SUBJECTS IN THE LIBRARY CATALOG

African American Authors

American Literature—African American Authors

American Literature—Women Authors

Walker, Alice

BROWSE FOR BOOKS ON THE SHELF USING THESE CALL NUMBERS

Biography section under Walker, Alice

810.8–818 (American Literature)

920 (Collected Biography)

REFERENCE MATERIALS THAT MAY HELP (BOOKS OR CD-ROMS)

DISCovering Authors. Gale Research, 1996. (CD-ROM)

Gates, Henry Louis, Jr., ed. *Bearing Witness: Selections from African-American Autobiography in the Twentieth Century*. Pantheon Books, 1991.

Malinowski, Sharon, ed. *Black Writers*. Gale Research, 1994.

Modern American Women Writers. Scribner, 1991.

Smith, Jessie Carney, ed. *Notable Black American Women, Book II*. Gale Research, 1996.

Smith, Valerie, et al., eds. *African American Writers*. Collier Books, 1993.

PERIODICAL INDEXES

Biography Index

EBSCO Magazine Article Summaries

InfoTrac

Reader's Guide to Periodical Literature

SUGGESTED INTERNET SITES

http://www.public.asu.edu/~metro/aflit/walker/index.html (Biography, bibliography, criticisms, and links)

http://www.luminarium.org/contemporary/alicew (Biography; bibliography; links to more biographies and bibliographies, interviews, essays, reviews, and excerpts from works)

KEY WORD FOR PERIODICAL AND ONLINE SEARCHES

Walker, Alice

VIDEO PROGRAMS RELATED TO THIS TOPIC

Alice Walker. Swiss Television, 1992.
Alice Walker: Author. Schlessinger Video, 1994.
The Color Purple. Warners.

ORGANIZATION TO CONTACT FOR ADDITIONAL INFORMATION

Alice Walker, c/o Joan Mira, 327 25th Avenue, #3, San Francisco, CA 94121. Phone: 415–750–9602, Fax: 415–750–9317.

SUGGESTIONS FOR NARROWING THIS TOPIC

Discuss how Alice Walker depicts black women in her novels and poetry.
Discuss the exploration of black-white relations in Walker's novel *Meridian*.
Research Walker's involvement in the Civil Rights Movement.
Write a biographical essay about Alice Walker, focusing on her childhood and its influences on her works.

RELATED TOPICS

Civil Rights Movement
Racism
Toni Morrison

This RESEARCH TOPIC GUIDE is intended to help you find information on your topic in a wide variety of sources in this and any other library. Resources, though, are not limited to those described and not all libraries will have the same titles. Please ask a librarian for further guidance.

Appendix: Research Topic Guide Template

Topic

BACKGROUND

LOOK UNDER THE FOLLOWING SUBJECTS IN THE LIBRARY CATALOG

BROWSE FOR BOOKS ON THE SHELF USING THESE CALL NUMBERS

REFERENCE MATERIALS THAT MAY HELP (BOOKS OR CD-ROMS)

PERIODICAL INDEXES

SUGGESTED INTERNET SITES

KEY WORDS FOR PERIODICAL AND ONLINE SEARCHES

VIDEO PROGRAMS RELATED TO THIS TOPIC

ORGANIZATIONS TO CONTACT FOR ADDITIONAL INFORMATION

SUGGESTIONS FOR NARROWING THIS TOPIC

RELATED TOPICS

This RESEARCH TOPIC GUIDE is intended to help you find information on your topic in a wide variety of sources in this and any other library. Resources, though, are not limited to those described and not all libraries will have the same titles. Please ask a librarian for further guidance.

Index

About the Author

DANA MCDOUGALD has taught all grade levels from Head Start to graduate students and has been a librarian at Cedar Shoals High School since 1979. She is co-author with Melvin Bowie of *Information Services for Secondary Schools* (Greenwood, 1997).